MICHIGAN BUSINESS STUDIES
Volume I Number 4
New Series

DYNAMIC CALL OPTION MODELS

Theory and Evidence

Richard J. Rogalski

Division of Research
Graduate School of Business Administration
The University of Michigan

ISBN 0-87712-184-2

A Publication of the
Division of Research
Graduate School of Business Administration
The University of Michigan
Ann Arbor, Michigan

Printed in the United States of America

To Midget, *amante*

CONTENTS

Foreword **xv**

Acknowledgments **xvii**

1. Introduction and Overview **1**

Stock Market Prices 1

An Introduction to Options 2

Current State of Option Theory 4

Preview of the Study 8

2. Economic Considerations **9**

Introduction 9

Investor Expectations 10

A Rationale for Expectations 10

Previous Theories 11

A Theory of Investor Behavior Under Uncertainty 12

Potential Surprise 15

Focus Outcomes 16

Investor Preference 18

Implications for Option Markets 19

The Postulated Dynamic Models 20

Assumptions 20

The Fundamental Dynamic Equation 21

The Behavioral Dynamic Equation 22

Purposes of This Investigation 24

3. Statistical Considerations **26**

Introduction 26

Random Functions 26

Autocovariance Functions 26

Stationary Random Functions 27

Autocorrelation Functions 27

Estimation of Autocorrelation Functions 27
Cross Covariance Functions 28
Cross Correlation Functions 28
Estimation of Cross Correlation Functions 28
White Noise 29
Dynamic Models 29
Two-Stage Identification 32
Parameter Estimates 35
Diagnostic Checks 37

4. Description of the Data and Hypotheses **39**
Types of Options 39
The Companies Selected 40
Types and Sources of Data 42
Prices 42
Volume 45
Volatility 46
Senior Security 47
Sources of Data 48
Univariate Series Analysis 48
Examples of Univariate Analysis 50
Warrant Series 50
Focus High Series 54
The Remaining Series 54

5. Data Analysis of the Fundamental Dynamic Equation **58**
Introduction 58
An Example of the Methodology 59
Relating the Two Series 60
Fitting the Model 60
Further Modeling 63
Checking the Model 64
Relationships Between Price and Focus Value 66
Fundamental Dynamic Equations 70
Results for Focus High 72
Results for Focus Low 80
Discussion of Results and Conclusions 80

6. Data Analysis of the Behavioral Dynamic Equation **85**
Introduction 85
Exogenous Influences 85

Price-Exogenous Relationships 86
Exogenous Interrelationships 91
Principal Components 91
Results of Principal Components Analysis 98
Estimated Autocorrelation Functions of the Principal Components 100
Independence of Principal Components 100
Relationships Between Warrants and Principal Components 100
Behavioral Dynamic Equations 106
The Methodology 106
An Example 108
Results for Focus High 111
Results for Focus Low 116
Discussion of Results and Conclusions 122
Summary 125

7. Summary and Suggestions for Future Research **126**
Summary 126
Suggestions for Further Research 126

Appendixes **129**
Appendix A. Means, Standard Deviations, and Coefficients of Variation of Data Series 131
Appendix B. Estimated Autocorrelations for Price Series 133
Appendix C. Relationships Between Price and Focus Value for Option Populations 137

Selected Bibliography **145**

TABLES

Table

1. The Option Population 41
2. Descriptions of the Selected Companies 43
3. Estimated Autocorrelations of the Price Series 54
4. Estimated Autocorrelations of the Exogenous Series . . . 55
5. Diagnostic Checks for Avco Example of Fundamental Dynamic Model 65
6. Relationships between Price and Focus Value 68
7. Fundamental Dynamic Models for Focus High 73
8. Residual Autocorrelations for Focus High Models Fitted in Table 7 75
9. Diagnostic Checks for Focus High Models Fitted in Table 7 . 76
10. Comparison of TWA (0, 1, 2) Models Fitted for Three Different Time Periods Before Maturity 77
11. Fundamental Dynamic Models for Focus Low 78
12. Residual Autocorrelations for Focus Low Models Fitted in Table 11 81
13. Diagnostic Checks for Focus Low Models Fitted in Table 11 . 82
14. Price-Exogenous Relationships 87
15. Exogenous Interrelationships 92
16. Correlation Coefficients of the Principal Components . . . 99
17. Estimated Autocorrelations of the Principal Components . . 101
18. Principal Component Interrelationships 102
19. Relationships between Warrants and Principal Components . 104
20. Diagnostic Checks for Avco Example of Behavioral Dynamic Model 110

21. Behavioral Dynamic Models for Focus High 113
22. Residual Autocorrelations for Focus High Models Fitted in Table 21 115
23. Diagnostic Checks for Focus High Models Fitted in Table 21 . 117
24. Behavioral Dynamic Models for Focus Low 118
25. Residual Autocorrelations for Focus Low Models Fitted in Table 24 120
26. Diagnostic Checks for Focus Low Models Fitted in Table 24 . 121

FIGURES

Figure

1. The Stock-Option Relationship 3
2. The Potential Surprise Curve 15
3. Focus Outcomes 17
4. Dynamic Expectations Hypothesis 23
5. Estimated Autocorrelations for Avco Series $y_c(t)$ 51
6. Estimated Autocorrelations for Avco Series $x_h(t)$ 52
7. Estimated Autocorrelations for Avco Series $\varepsilon(t:x_h)$ 53
8. Estimated Cross Correlation Function $r_k[\varepsilon(t:x_h);\ \varepsilon(t:y_c)]$ for Avco Corporation 61
9. Estimated Cross Correlation Function $r_k[\varepsilon(t+1:x_h);\ \varepsilon(t:y_c)]$ for Avco Corporation 62
10. Fitted Fundamental Dynamic Model for Avco Example . . 67
11. Illustrative Response Functions 71
12. Fitted Behavioral Dynamic Model for Avco Example . . . 112

FOREWORD

The basis for the research in Rogalski's book was a Ph.D. dissertation in Business Administration at the University of Michigan. This research represents original scholarship in all aspects. The research design, construction of the data base, methodological development and the statistical analyses are outstanding. This opinion was verified when the Selection Committee of the American Institute of Decision Sciences (AIDS), under the Chairmanship of Professor Charles P. Bonini of Stanford University, judged Rogalski's dissertation to be one of the four chosen as "outstanding" in the 1975 national competition.

The research makes a significant contribution to the theoretical understanding of option price behavior. The research findings, as well as the methodological approach used to develop them, are of fundamental importance for the analysis of option price behavior. The application of discrete linear stochastic processes of the autoregressive–moving average type presented in this volume, as well as the underlying investment rationale that suggests the application of such stochastic processes, are unique in the field today.

The members of Rogalski's dissertation committee—Professors Dick A. Leabo and William J. Wrobleski, co-chairmen, Professor James N. Morgan and Professor C. James Pilcher—join in commending this research to all those interested in the fascinating and growing area of financial analysis.

Dick A. Leabo
William J. Wrobleski

Ann Arbor, Michigan

ACKNOWLEDGMENTS

Professors Dick A. Leabo and William J. Wrobleski of the University of Michigan Graduate School of Business Administration guided this research from inception to conclusion. Professor James W. Morgan of the Economics Department and the Institute for Social Research also spent much time providing valuable criticisms and suggestions. I also thank Timothy J. Nantell for his thoughtful comments and discussions.

I appreciate the editorial assistance of Joan Kmenta at the Division of Research, Graduate School of Business Administration, University of Michigan. Finally, the patience, understanding, and encouragement of my wife, Marjorie, will always be remembered.

R. J. R.

1

INTRODUCTION AND OVERVIEW

Stock Market Prices

The past decade has seen renewed interest by economists in the operations of the stock market. Advances have been made in such subjects as the formulation of capital asset prices, portfolio selection, capital budgeting, efficient capital markets, and other areas. A common characteristic of work in these areas has been the development of security models that analyze the role of risk and of expectations in investment decisions.

The results of all activities of the stock market are primarily reflected in recorded price movements. Price is the causal mechanism through which economists traditionally have studied market interactions. Shifts in investor preferences, technological innovations, and psychological factors (whether temporary or permanent) eventually manifest themselves to some extent through price. Economists recognized that a multiplicity of economic variables will influence price, and they have attempted to formulate models of market behavior that explicitly consider the net effect of such changes.

One goal of this study will be to extend the traditional synthesis mentioned above by developing behavioral models of price change. Recent advances in the theory of multiple time series will provide a methodology for identifying the dynamic interrelationships of price, expectations, risk, and other market factors. Such an undertaking, it is hoped, would be beneficial in two respects. First, it should determine some of the underlying causes of price movements. Second, the insights gained by such identification may lead to new or improved methodologies.

An example of the benefits which may accrue is provided by the critical dependence of prices on expectations. More precisely, the way investors form their expectations of which prices will prevail in the market substantially influences price over time. A major obstacle for empirical investigators has been a lack of knowledge about how expectations are formed and how they operate on the stock market. One of the principal tasks of this study will be to introduce expectations explicitly into the determination of price behavior.

An Introduction to Options

As the title of this book indicates, the realm of this study is limited to a particular type of capital instrument—the option. An option is a security giving one the right to buy or sell an asset. This study will be concerned only with the kind of option that gives one the right to buy a single share of common stock. The owner is entitled to exchange the option for the stock within a specified time period at a stipulated price, termed the exercise price (or striking price).

In general, the higher the price of the common stock, the greater the value of the option. Normally the value of an option declines as its maturity date approaches, providing the value of the stock does not change. The general properties of the relation between the option value and the stock price are often illustrated in a diagram like Figure 1. The upper bound represents the maximum value of the option. It cannot exceed the value of the stock because the option is inferior to the stock with respect to dividends, voting power, and length of life. In contrast, an option cannot sell for less than the difference between the price of the stock and the exercise price S. This lower bound, which represents the theoretical value of an option, is defended by arbitrageurs, for if the option could be purchased for less, a simultaneous short sale of the stock would yield an instantaneous and riskless profit.

The curve representing the value of an option will usually be convex. When the price of the stock is high in relation to the exercise price, the value of an option approaches its theoretical value. Because the curve will also lie below the upper bound (represented by a 45° line) the option will be more volatile than the stock. A given percentage change in the stock will result in a larger percentage change in the option value.[1]

There are two concepts of time inherent in Figure 1. The first concerns the maturity date. Lines V_1, V_2, V_3 represent the value of an option for successively shorter maturities. The shorter the period to maturity, the more convex the relationship and the more it approaches the lower bound. When the maturity date is further away, the curve becomes flatter and higher. To understand the second notion of time, it is necessary to hold maturity constant. Then one of the curves, say V_2,

1. This is the concept of leverage. The most essential feature of leverage is that the higher the amount of leverage an asset has, the greater the risk or uncertainty in the price of that asset.

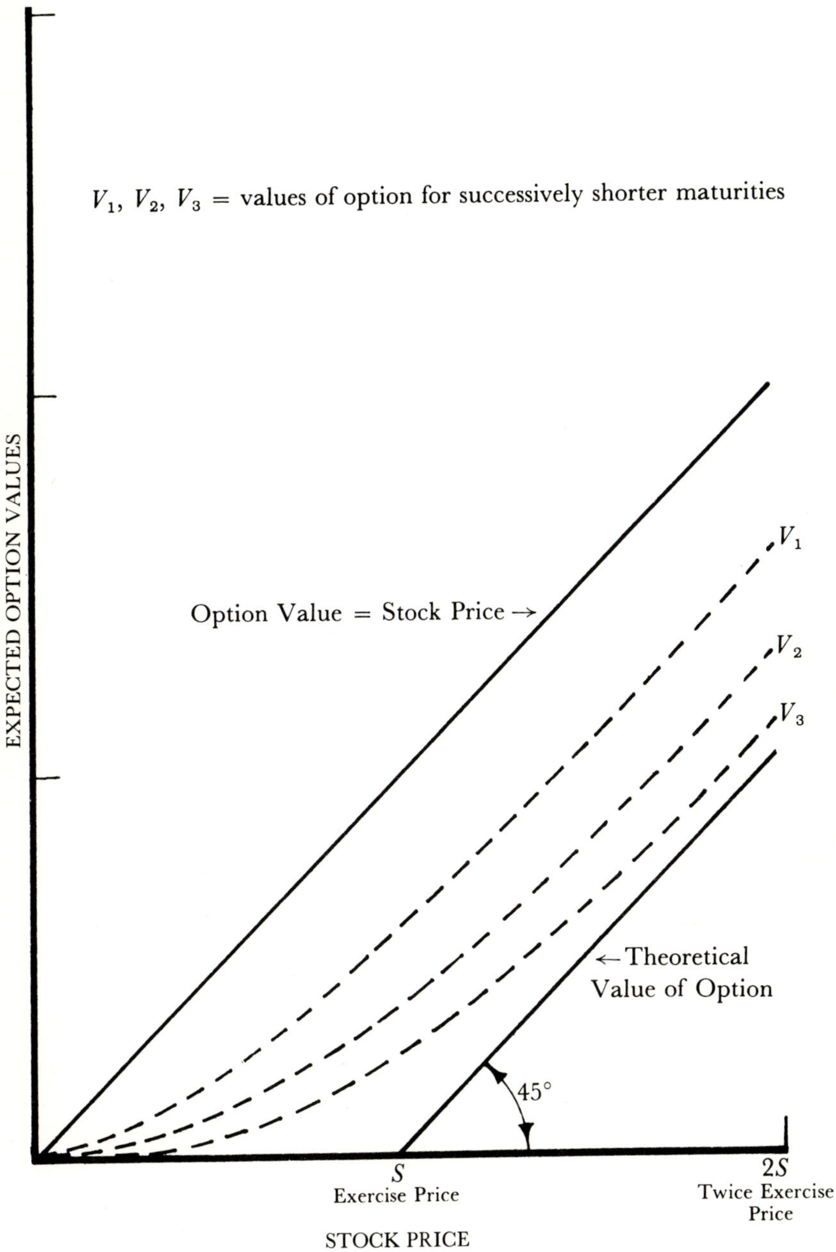

Fig. 1 The stock-option relationship

represents the value of an option for a given period. The value of an option, however, has been at different positions along this curve at various times.

Current State of Option Theory[2]

It is generally recognized that the future value of a random variable y representing the value of an option is a function of the future price of its associated stock at maturity x; the probability distribution of $x, f(x)$; and the exercise price S. At expiration the value of the option is

$$\begin{array}{ll} (x - S) & \text{if } x > S \\ 0 & \text{if } x \leqq S. \end{array}$$

If $f(x)$ is continuous, the expected future value of the option at expiration is

$$E[y] = \int_S^{\infty} (x - S) f(x) dx. \tag{1.1}$$

To use equation (1.1) it is necessary to make some assumptions about the form of $f(x)$. The typical assumption made is that the distribution of stock returns is well approximated by a normal distribution. This return-generating process is an unbounded random walk with a trend, where the trend may be thought of as the expected growth rate of the stock. It is argued that if stock prices actually follow a log normal random walk, then it is reasonable to assume that investors think future returns are log normal. A normal distribution of expected returns is further rationalized by assuming that an investor thinks percentage rises or drops in prices are important. Then the size of the rise or drop depends on the current price of the stock.

Sprenkle (1961), Boness (1964), Samuelson (1965a), Chen (1970), and others have all produced valuation formulas from using equation (1.1).[3] The model of Sprenkle will illustrate the typical analysis. Sprenkle assumes that the distribution of possible values of the stock at maturity is log normal, and then he determines the expected value of an option given

2. An excellent review of option pricing theory is contained in Smith (1976). This section is only an attempt to highlight the state of the art.

3. Most of the previous work on options has been expressed in terms of warrants, but the more general term *option* is preferred for this discussion.

the current stock price as

$$(1.2) \quad E[y|x_*] = e^{\rho T} S \cdot N\left\{\frac{\ln(S/X) + [\rho + (\sigma^2/2)]T}{\sigma\sqrt{T}}\right\} - (1 - k)X \cdot N\left\{\frac{\ln(S/X) + [\rho - (\sigma^2/2)]T}{\sigma\sqrt{T}}\right\},$$

where e represents an exponential, *ln* the natural logarithms, ρ is the expected average rate of growth in the stock price S, T is the time to expiration, X is the exercise price, σ^2 is the variance rate of stock returns, and k is an adjustment for the degree of market risk aversion.

Both of the $N\{*\}$ are standardized normal distributions, so that once the limits * are computed, their values are easily obtained from tables. To use this formula one needs to determine an appropriate discount rate ρ and the variance of stock returns σ^2. A good estimate for σ^2 can usually be obtained from past data, given the log normal assumption. By contrast, the problem of estimating ρ from past data is very difficult.

Samuelson (1965a) was the first to observe that equation (1.1) is only applicable to options at maturity, hence neglecting the important fact that options are exercisable prior to maturity.[4] He assumes that (1) stock prices have a constant expected growth rate α per unit of time, (2) option prices have a constant expected growth rate β per unit of time, (3) $(\beta - \alpha) \geqq 0$, and (4) the distribution of stock prices at maturity is log normal. He then determines the value of an option by discounting the expected value to present at the rate β. In a subsequent paper Samuelson and Merton (1969) modify the contention that $(\beta - \alpha) \geqq 0$ must be a constant. They advance the theory by treating $(\beta - \alpha)$ as a function of the stock price, the dividend yield of the stock, and the time until maturity.

Additional studies using Samuelson's (1965a) rational theory as a base have centered on the problem of deciding when to exercise an option. Chen (1970), Stone (1970), and Chopra (1973) have modeled the problem of finding the optimal policy for exercising an option in terms of the "stopping rule" problem of dynamic programming. It is assumed that investors make decisions with an objective of maximizing the expected value of an option. Then an investor has two choices at each period; he may (1) exercise the option or (2) hold the option one more period and then make the optimal decision.

4. Note that if one removes the assumption of price expectations only for a specific future date in equation (1.1), the problem of valuation becomes quite complicated. The investor is now able to hold the option for any length of time up to maturity. A major problem would then exist to estimate possible stock prices in a number of future periods.

Leabo and Rogalski (1974) were the first to explicitly test the validity of the random walk theory for options. Within the context of market efficiency, their work can best be described as a weak form test in which the information set is only historical prices. Their results indicate the presence of significant and negative linear dependence between lagged price changes or returns. They advance the theory by explaining the observed nonrandomness in terms of a random walk model between reflecting barriers.[5]

In a recent paper Black and Scholes (1973) established a model for determining the equilibrium value of an option. They derive the model using the capital asset pricing model first developed by Sharpe (1964). The capital asset pricing model is a general equilibrium model of the pricing of securities that describes the relation between risk and expected returns for a capital asset. More specifically, the expected return on a security $E[R_i]$ above a risk-free rate r is proportional to its systematic risk β_i

$$E[R_i] - r = \beta_i\{E[R_m] - r\}, \tag{1.3}$$

where the expected risk premium on the market is $\{E[R_m] - r\}$.

Using the asset pricing model, Black and Scholes find an option value such that the option and stock are always in equilibrium. Although the same relationship in (1.3) must be true for an option, the beta of the option is constantly changing because of leverage. At high stock prices the beta of the option approaches the beta of the stock because the option becomes more like the stock. At low stock prices the beta of the option will be greater than the beta of the stock. From this argument Black and Scholes conclude that the beta of the stock is not an appropriate discount rate because the option value changes as a function of the stock price and time.

In contrast to the earlier work of Sprenkle and others, Black and Scholes have shown that the appropriate discount rate to use is r. They reason that because there is an exact relationship between the stock price and the option price, an investor can create a hedged position by going long in one security and short in the other to create a neutral risk situation. However, he will have to earn the risk-free rate on his investment because, in equilibrium, the expected return on a hedged position must be equal to the risk-free rate. The Black and Scholes general equilibrium solution

5. Empirical evidence has supported the theory of options presented in this section. In particular, studies by Kassouf (1965), Shelton (1967), Van Horne (1969), and Melicher and Rush (1974) are in general agreement that option price is significantly and positively related to stock price and to time until maturity, and negatively related to dividend yield.

to the call pricing problem can be written as

$$(1.4) \qquad E[y|x_*] = S \cdot N\left\{\frac{\ln(S/X) + [r + (\sigma^2/2)T]}{\sigma\sqrt{T}}\right\} - e^{-rT}X \cdot N\left\{\frac{\ln(S/X) + [r - (\sigma^2/2)]T}{\sigma\sqrt{T}}\right\},$$

where r is the risk-free interest rate and all other variables are as defined in equation (1.2).

Thus, Black and Scholes have shown that the value of an option is primarily a function of the borrowing rate in the market and the variance rate of stock returns. Once values for these two parameters are known, equation (1.4) can be used to determine an option's value. For options of short duration the interest rate can be assumed constant or estimated by using a short-term market instrument comparable in maturity to the option. The variance rate of the stock returns must still be estimated from past data.

Finally, an extension of the Black and Scholes model is currently being researched—a jump process for stock price movements. Cox and Ross (1975) demonstrate that the log normal process of Black and Scholes is a special case of their simple jump process. If stock prices jump in only one direction and the jumps are of a constant amplitude, then the Black–Scholes hedge can be created, and the option price determined as

$$(1.5a) \qquad E[y|x_*] = S \cdot F\left\{\frac{2(r - \mu)kT}{k - 1}; \frac{2\ln(X/S) - 2\mu T}{\ln k} + 2\right\} - Xe^{-rT}F\left\{\frac{2y}{k}; \frac{2\ln(X/S) - 2\mu T}{\ln k} + 2\right\}$$

if the jumps are in an upward direction, i.e. $k > 1$, and as

$$(1.5b) \qquad E[y|x_*] = S \cdot G\left\{\frac{2(r - \mu)kT}{k - 1}; \frac{2\ln(X/S) - 2\mu T}{\ln k} + 2\right\} - Xe^{-rT}G\left\{\frac{2y}{k}; \frac{2\ln(X/S) - 2\mu T}{\ln k} + 2\right\}$$

if the jumps are in a downward direction, i.e. $k < 1$, where μ is the expected return on the stock, k is the direction of the jump, and all other variables are as defined in equation (1.2). $F\{*, **\}$ and $G\{*, **\}$ are the cumulative and complementary chi-square distributions for ** degrees of freedom. It is important to note that if stock prices follow a simple jump process, then stock return expectations are needed to price call options correctly.

Preview of the Study

This book will be composed of seven chapters. Chapter 2 is a brief review of alternate economic theories of price expectations. Given a few general assumptions about investor behavior, the theory of Shackle (1961) is used to derive a fundamental dynamic equation to represent the option pricing process. This model is generalized to a behavioral dynamic equation which includes several price determinants.

In Chapter 3, certain definitions and fundamental concepts are discussed that are basic to an understanding of the analysis to follow. The modeling procedures of Box and Jenkins (1970) based on rational lag functions are introduced. Each of the three stages of their iterative method—identification, estimation, and diagnostic checking—will be described.

Chapter 4 outlines the types and sources of data collected. A rationale is given for each time series. Examples illustrate the data transformations. The primary empirical results of the study, presented in Chapters 5 and 6, were obtained by application of new statistical methods to analyze the data.

Using a fundamental dynamic equation, Chapter 5 illustrates how various expectations hypotheses can be tested by applying the recent developments of Box and Jenkins. The results of these investigations suggest that investor expectations of stock price are positively related to option value.

Chapter 6 extends the analysis of Chapter 5 to include several exogenous variables. The specification of market interrelationships is highlighted. In addition to expectations, it is concluded that psychological forces in the market as well as interest rate risk are dominant factors in option price formation.

Chapter 7 summarizes the results and suggests areas of future research.

2

ECONOMIC CONSIDERATIONS

Introduction

The current theory of options formally acknowledges that the expected return of an option will depend on the expected return of the stock. An important implication of this theory is that the price of an option may be positively related to investor expectations of the associated stock.

Although this association has been recognized, the difficulty in quantifying expectations has resulted in the acceptance of option valuation models that tend to ignore the direct influence of expectations. For example, the Black and Scholes model (1973), which does not include an expectations term, has gained popularity in the investment community. But if more general models such as the one by Cox and Ross (1975) are to be implemented, then stock return expectations must somehow be quantified.

At least three studies have empirically examined the topic of expectations in terms of the relation between stock price drift and option price. Sprenkle (1961) attempted to identify and estimate investor expectations, but was unable to do so. Shelton (1967) concluded that no such relationship existed. Kassouf (1965) found a significant relationship. His results are consistent with a time lag in the adjustment of option price to stock price. This implies that the price of an option is partially determined by how the stock arrived at its present level.

The purpose of this chapter will be to formulate an expectations model for options under the assumption that option price and stock expectations are positively related. This chapter begins by reviewing previous economic theories of price expectations. Then a theory of investor behavior under uncertainty will be discussed in light of Shackle's work (1961). Finally, a class of dynamic models is postulated within the framework of Shackle's hypothesis.

Investor Expectations

In this thesis the term *expectations* shall always refer to *investor expectations* and will be interpreted as anticipation of the future. It is the mental process of creating possible situations and associating them with future dates. Each of these situations is assigned a degree of belief that specified behavior will make the hypothesis come true.

A Rationale for Expectations

Suppose that as a gift you receive an option with the privilege to buy XYZ common stock at \$15 and XYZ common happens to be selling in the market at \$10. The theoretical value of the option is zero. On this basis you consider the option worthless and discard it. Now, suppose that XYZ common stock had a reasonably good chance to reach a high price level in the future. More precisely, one year later the price of XYZ common rises to \$20. The option you discarded turned out to be worth something after all. The market price of an option, then, may be greater than zero even though its theoretical value is zero. This additional value is often referred to as the privilege of an option and represents the right to buy a share of the stock at some future date.

Any investment decision implies a forecast of future events. The main point of the above discussion is that option value is dependent upon investor responses to changes in the expected level of stock prices. Consider a pair of time series $y(t)$, $x_e(t)$ where $y(t)$ is the price of an option as valued by an investor at time t and let $y(t)$ be causally related only to $x_e(t)$, where x represents investor expectations of stock price formed at time t. It can be postulated that the ordering of such series in time leads one to an investigation of possible dependence among values:

$$y(t) = \beta x_e(t), \tag{2.1}$$

where β is a function of the expected rate of return on the option.

Now, on the average, it is investor valuation that determines the market price of an option. For an individual investor it is reasonable to assume that investment decisions are based on an explicit or implicit time horizon. For average investor behavior one must assume that the longest individual time horizon will dominate. It is also possible that some investor expectations are not realized, which may cause previous expectations to influence valuation. This argument asserts that the option price as valued by investors on the average may be formulated as

$$y(t) = \sum_{s=-b_1}^{b_2} \beta_s x_e(t - s) + \varepsilon(t), \tag{2.2a}$$

where β_s is an unknown lag function for periods $s = -b_1, \ldots, b_2$ and $\varepsilon(t)$ is an error term assumed normal with constant variance that measures the random effect of other factors.

Taking expected values of each side of equation (2.2a) yields

$$E[y(t)|x_e] = \sum_{s=-b_1}^{b_2} \beta_s x_e(t-s). \tag{2.2b}$$

Equation (2.2b) states that $y(t)$ over all traders in the market is a weighted sum of past and anticipated stock price expectations. The weights β_s, applied in forming the expectations, depend upon investor resources and investor confidence in their expectations.

Previous Theories

It should be noted that equation (2.2) is not operational in terms of estimating β_s unless one assumes how expectations are formed, because x_e is not observable. Several theories concerning the form of x_e have been proposed. Most of these theories rely on past prices and are of little use in speculative markets. Therefore, these theories will only be outlined to give the reader a flavor for attempts to quantify $x_e(t)$. The next section will develop an alternative theory of expectations.

Static Expectations

A naive form of expectations originally used by Ezekiel (1938) in the cobweb model is

$$x_e(t) = x(t-1), \tag{2.3}$$

in which expectations are equal to the latest known stock price.

Extrapolative Expectations

Goodwin (1947) proposed the following formula:

$$x_e(t) = x(t-1) + \alpha[x(t-1) - x(t-2)], \qquad -1 < \alpha < 1. \tag{2.4}$$

That is, a certain fraction of the latest change is added to the most recently observed stock price. A variety of behavior can be obtained depending on the sign of α.

Adaptive Expectations

The adaptive expectations model proposed by Nerlove (1958) satisfies the following equation:

$$x_e(t) = x_e(t-1) + \alpha[x(t-1) - x_e(t-1)] \tag{2.5}$$

with $0 \leqq \alpha \leqq 1$. Under this assumption, expectations are revised each period in proportion to the difference between the current stock price and the previous expectation. If α were equal to zero, the current stock price would have no effect on expectations. The case $\alpha = 1$ corresponds to the static model.

Rational Expectations

Muth (1961) has argued that the anticipated price $x_e(t)$ should equal the statistically expected price. More precisely, he proposed that price be a linear function of independent disturbances so that

$$x(t) = \sum_{i=0}^{\infty} w_i \varepsilon(t - i), \tag{2.6}$$

where the ε's are normally and independently distributed random variates with constant variance. Anticipated price will also be the same weighted linear function based on information available at the end of the previous period:

$$x_e(t) = \sum_{i=1}^{\infty} w_i \varepsilon(t - i), \tag{2.7}$$

implying that

$$x(t) = x_e(t) + w_0 \varepsilon(t). \tag{2.8}$$

Taking expected values gives the model

$$x_e(t) = E[x(t)]. \tag{2.9}$$

One implication of this hypothesis is simply that readily available information will not be wasted. The rational hypothesis further implies that a sequence of anticipated prices follows a martingale,[1] as formally shown by Samuelson (1965b).

A Theory of Investor Behavior Under Uncertainty

That uncertainty affects investment decisions is well known. These decisions are made by choosing among alternative courses of action which have uncertain outcomes. These alternative courses of action will have

1. If the expected value of the next period's price as projected on the basis of a given information set is *equal* to the current price, then the price sequence follows a martingale.

differing amounts of uncertainty or risk.[2] Because it is impossible to know for certain what will happen in the future, investment decisions can only be based on what is expected to happen.

A theory of uncertainty for options must deal with two distinct forms of investor behavior. First of all, it must be concerned with the manner in which an investor summarizes his views about the future course of events. In general one must suppose that to form such views he partially draws upon market information and his own personal experiences of the past. The second part of any theory must be able to describe the behavior of the investor, given a set of expectations. In order to do this, a general motive must be ascribed to investors.

Consider an investor who must decide at various discrete points in his lifetime what portion of his wealth will be consumed and what portion invested. The investor is assumed to derive satisfaction only from consumption. That portion invested is expected to increase future wealth, which in turn will be allocated to consumption and investment. The investor's problem is to determine an optimal consumption–investment sequence that maximizes his level of satisfaction provided by anticipated consumption.

The generally accepted solution to the problem is to assume that the theory of choice followed by an investor conforms to the expected utility hypothesis.[3] Expected utility is determined on the basis of the probability distribution of possible outcomes of an investment. The expected utility hypothesis states that an investor examines the expected utility associated with every possible consumption–investment decision and chooses the one that maximizes expected utility.

In principle the hypothesis is a complete theory of choice, but in practice the process provides no testable propositions about investor behavior. To give the problem structure, it is usually assumed that an investor is able to summarize his beliefs about the probability distribution of possible outcomes of an investment in terms of two parameters of the distribution. These parameters are the mean or expected value and some measure of dispersion, usually the standard deviation. Thus, expected utility is expressed as a function of two parameters as opposed to the entire distribution of possible outcomes.[4]

2. The terms *risk* and *uncertainty* are sometimes given different meanings. A situation of risk is said to exist if an investor is willing to base his action on a probability distribution. Otherwise, there is either certainty or uncertainty. In this thesis, the terms risk and uncertainty will be used synonymously.

3. Von Neuman and Morgenstern (1947) are responsible for extending the theory of choice under uncertainty to problems involving expectations by the assumption that individuals maximize expected wealth.

4. Fama and Merton (1972) give an excellent discussion of the mean–standard deviation model.

There are a number of difficulties associated with such an approach. First, the form of the distribution is a major factor in determining the riskiness of an investment. For example, although two different distributions may have the same mean, the probability of very large changes may be much greater for one than the other. To the extent that investors prefer one of the distributions to the other, the standard deviation is not a sufficient measure of risk. Second, only for symmetric distributions (in which the shape of the distribution is known) can this two-parameter approach approximate investor attitudes toward risk. In this special case, greater dispersion would consistently represent greater riskiness, other things remaining equal. Finally, the procedure of calculating the standard deviation is to square and add the deviations on both sides of the mean. Most investors feel that deviations above expected outcomes are desirable rather than undesirable.

For the above reasons it will be assumed in this thesis that investors determine expected utility to be derived from an investment on the basis of two "distribution free" values. The basic premise is that any uncertainty situation can be reduced to two relevant outcomes. At any given point in time an investor is assumed to focus his attention on only the two extremes of the distribution of all possible outcomes. These values do not depend on the distribution from which the random sample of outcomes is obtained, and the values may be considered as extremes of an order statistic.

To illustrate the basic model, consider the situation where all possible expected returns to an investor are known with certainty. Uncertainty then plays no part in the selection of outcomes; the selection depends upon the outcomes' desirability to the investor. In this case, only two outcomes are relevant to the investor, namely, the best and the worst, or the two extremes of the possible outcomes ordered according to their desirability. Under these circumstances, an investor would not be concerned with a moderately good outcome if an excellent one were equally possible. On the other hand, he would not consider a moderately bad outcome if complete loss of his investment were equally possible. In sum, an investor is able to rank the distributions of outcomes on the basis of two values: the worst and the best possible outcomes.

Generalization of this basic model involves including different degrees of uncertainty or possibility. Investment selection would then depend upon the utility for money at various levels of possibility. The remainder of this section will define the properties comprising this theory of uncertainty. The material to be presented is a summary of the theory of expectations developed by Shackle and adapted here to options.[5]

5. For a complete discussion of the theory to be presented, the reader is referred to Shackle (1961).

Potential Surprise

A hypothetical outcome of the stock price shall refer to an imagined segment of the future limited by some horizon period. It is upon this complex entity and its relation with what an investor knows or perceives about the marketplace (including its psychological patterns) that investor judgments of potential surprise are based. The potential surprise attached to an outcome is defined as the surprise that the investor would experience if that outcome actually resulted.

A specific type of curve can be drawn to represent potential surprise as a function of hypothetical stock prices. Let *PS* refer to the degree of potential surprise associated with a continuous variable x which represents future stock price outcomes. Any combination of stock price and the potential surprise of that price, denoted (x, PS), will be termed an expectation element. A graph of the potential surprise curve $PS = g(x)$ will typically resemble Figure 2.

The fixed price x_* will be the current stock price. An outcome can

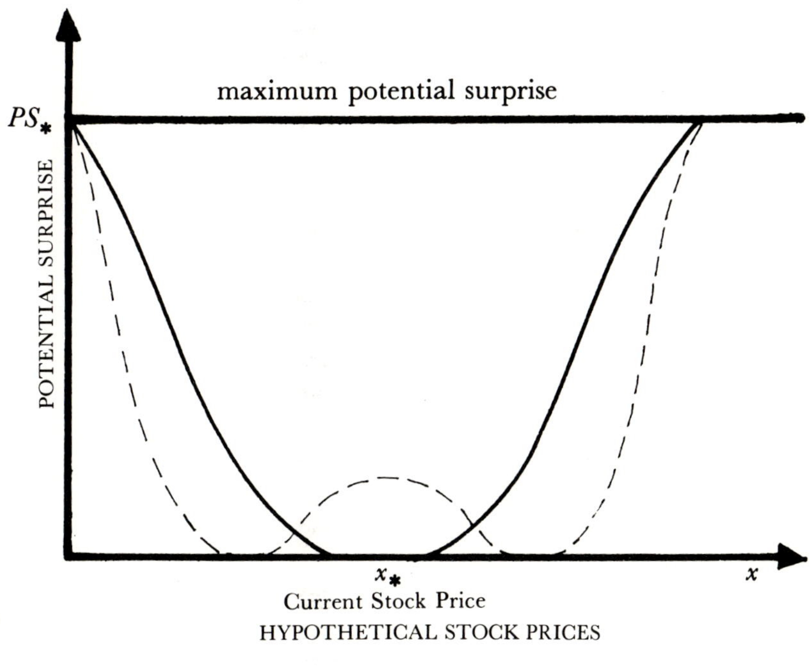

Fig. 2 The potential surprise curve

now be interpreted as placing an investor in a worse or better position than he is in currently. Above and below x_* it is assumed that PS will increase (decrease) with the numerical increase (decrease) of x.[6] There will be two values of x at which PS is a maximum (minimum), $PS = PS_*$, beyond which future stock prices will seem to an investor either too good or too bad to be true.

It should be noted that there can be many variations and modifications of this graph. To illustrate, consider the dotted line in Figure 2. The shape of this potential surprise curve implies that an investment will yield either a substantial gain or a substantial loss. This sort of expectation might be more appropriate for options because of their leverage.[7]

Finally, a potential surprise curve may provide an explanation of the degree of risk attached to an investment.[8] It might be assumed that the smaller the area enclosed by the potential surprise curve, the more confident an investor's expectation. Thus, the degree of risk an investor attaches to an investment may be thought to be a ratio of the area to the left of x_* to the total area.

Focus Outcomes

Let $\Phi = h\{x, g(t)\}$ denote a real function connecting the characteristics of an expectation element with the relevance of the element to an investor. Thus, one element can be assigned a higher value of this function than another element. The values of the function serve to select the element upon which an investor's attention will be concentrated.

The ascendency function Φ simply represents a type of trade-off encompassing possibility and desirability. A future stock price loses ascendency by seeming to the investor less than perfectly possible; it gains ascendency by approaching perfect possibility. The surface will only be defined for the interval $0 \leqq PS \leqq PS_*$ because no meaning is attached to potential surprise beyond this range. Outcomes that an investor considers impossible will have no relevance for him, so that Φ will be zero everywhere on the line $PS = PS_*$.

Assume with respect to x_* that (1) a large increase in the stock price is more relevant to an investor than a smaller increase, so that

$$\frac{\partial \Phi}{\partial x} > 0 \quad \text{for all } x > x_*; \tag{2.10}$$

6. It should be noted that the x-axis could have been labeled expected return. Then, movements to the right of x_* represent a positive return while movements to the left of x_* represent a negative return.

7. The presentation will continue with Shackle's (1961) standard form of the potential surprise curve, remembering that many generalizations exist.

8. This idea of risk in terms of a potential surprise curve originated with Egerton (1960).

(2) a large stock price decrease is more relevant to an investor than a smaller decrease, so that

$$(2.11) \qquad \frac{\partial \Phi}{\partial x} < 0 \quad \text{for all } x < x_*;$$

and (3) a more likely future price is more relevant than a less likely one, so that

$$(2.12) \qquad \frac{\partial \Phi}{\partial PS} < 0 \quad \text{for all } 0 \leqq PS \leqq PS_*.$$

Based on these assumptions, it is argued by Shackle that the general shape of Φ can be drawn as in Figure 3. Both the ascendency function and the potential surprise curve have the same two axes and may be drawn on the same figure. By moving along the x-axis in either direction from x_*, successively higher contour lines are passed, representing higher values of Φ. To move away from the x-axis along any one of the contour lines would be to move toward higher values of x and PS. In order that Φ may be

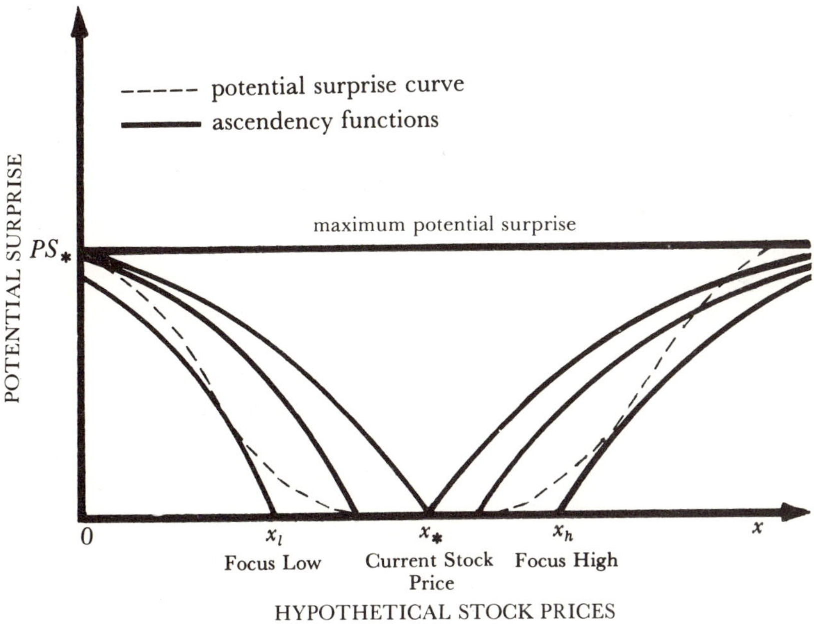

Fig. 3 Focus outcomes

constant, PS must increase to compensate for the effect of increasing x. No contour lines except $\Phi = 0$ can actually attain the line $PS = PS_*$ because of the assumption $h\{x, PS_*\} = 0$. Thus, each contour line will be concave to the x-axis and will approach the line $PS = PS_*$ asymptotically.

A focus outcome is defined as an expectation element which is special in the sense that it has power to concentrate an investor's attention upon itself. More formally, a primary focus outcome is defined as the maxima of the curve $\Phi = h\{x, f(x)\}$. It has been shown by Shackle that the maxima of Φ will occur at the point where the potential surprise curve is tangent to the contour lines as in Figure 3. Whenever the potential surprise curve is crossing contour lines, a movement along the curve brings one to successively higher (lower) values of Φ; a maximum can only occur where the potential surprise curve is not crossing the contour lines.

A problem with this approach is that the degree of potential surprise associated with each primary focus value is not the same. Shackle argues that it is necessary to eliminate the element of potential surprise before any comparison is possible. The resulting outcomes associated with zero potential surprise are just as relevant as the primary focus values. There is a one-to-one correspondence between these standardized focus outcomes and Φ. For expositional ease, the word standardized will be omitted in later discussions.

A Digression

Although it has been implied throughout the above discussion that profit and loss coexist in an investor's mind, they are in general mutually independent. A more realistic approach might have been to treat gains and losses separately, to allow for investor perception of their economic distinctions. The reason for showing both focus values on the same graph was nothing more than the convenience of using one diagram. Separate curves could have been drawn for each focus value. Therefore, the focus values will be distinguished for later reference by the terms focus low and focus high, denoted x_l, x_h, depending on their position to x_*. By making this distinction explicit, one can examine the factors which affect one and not the other. This may enable us to distinguish some of the complexities of the market for options.

Investor Preference

The focus value approach implies that uncertainty is the possibility that desired rather than expected outcomes will not be realized. Investors are presumed to have preferences regarding the future state of the stock. The value which an investor sets on an option is a function of two values. These two values represent the hope of gain and the fear of loss.

Assume that an investor views the outcomes of any investment in probabilistic terms; that is, he thinks of the possible results in terms of some probability distribution. In assessing the desirability of a particular investment, however, he is willing to act on the basis of two values—the focus low and focus high. Although these pairs are nondistributional, it is implied that each pair could be used to summarize a probability distribution of outcomes. This can be represented by a total utility function of the form

$$U = f(x_h, x_l), \tag{2.13}$$

where x_h indicates the standardized focus high and x_l the standardized focus low.

The theory assumes that any investor would consider investments with the same x_l and the same x_h equivalent. The following rules are assumed to apply to any investor:

1. If two investments have the same focus low but different focus highs, the one with the larger focus high is preferred.
2. If two investments have the same focus high but different focus lows, the one with the smaller focus low is preferred.
3. If an investment has a smaller focus low and a larger focus high than another, it is preferred.

Implicit in these rules is the assumption of risk aversion. Almost everyone is a risk averter when making important decisions. The feelings of a particular investor can usefully be represented by a family of indifference curves. As long as x_h is desired and x_l is not, every indifference curve will be upward-sloping. Generally, each curve will become steeper as x_h and x_l increase.

Implications for Option Markets

It is assumed that these focus prices apply to all option investors. Each investor will have an ascendency curve Φ and a value of x corresponding to a focus low and a focus high. Different investors will seek out and use different sets of available information. Anticipating events requires investors to obtain information to guide their actions. Investors, therefore, find themselves often of different opinion; one may be buying at the same time one is selling.

Now, in order to understand the trading process, we interpret the focus outcomes in terms of expected returns. Here x_* means a zero return;

the focus low, a negative return; and the focus high, a positive return. These two values can then be summed, yielding a net return. The marginal investor is just ready to buy or sell in the market. If he buys, he presumably thinks that his focus high is just sufficient to compensate his focus low, meaning a positive net return. The marginal investor who sells to him presumably thinks that his net return is negative. For each individual sale the actual investors who buy and sell will usually be different, but the decision-making process as described by focus values remains the same. Actual market prices over a given period will then reflect the consensus of marginal investors' opinions (based on available market information) as to focus values.

The Postulated Dynamic Models

The fact of uncertainty is not recognized in static economic theory, which deals with absolute quantities. There the time element is ignored, and the conditions of equilibrium are demonstrated without reference to the passage of time. This implies that the adaptation process does not itself influence the equilibrium conditions. However, prices in competitive markets do change in time; and a dynamic theory, in contrast with static theory, is necessary to attempt to analyze and explain this time movement. With change through time comes uncertainty because future prices are unknown. Because present market behavior affects future market prices and vice versa, there must be some sort of expectation about the uncertain future before investors act. The introduction of expectations, though, does not of itself create a dynamic theory. A dynamic theory must show how the present creates the future as well as how the future affects the present. That involves a knowledge of how expectations are formed in relation to many additional factors.

Assumptions

The term dynamic shall mean a scheme of inference such that, when the situation at each of certain dates is specified, the situation at one or more other dates can be determined. Note that the words *past* or *future* have not been used in this definition. They were not needed since *dynamic* in the strictest sense is independent of the notion of past and future, except when inferences may have to proceed from earlier to later or vice versa. In developing dynamic models for the value of an option, certain conditions will be assumed.

Assumption 1: The discount rate used to represent the value of money remains unchanged over investor horizon periods.

Assumption 2: The option is regarded as having 100 percent positive correlation with its stock. This is reasonable because options pay no dividends and have no vote nor claim to earnings. They represent solely a claim to the stock.

Assumption 3: Actual market prices of options over a given period will reflect the consensus of marginal investor opinions (based on available market information) as to focus values of stock outcomes.

Assumption 4: Investors follow a dynamic decision process in the sense that if expectations (and other factors) at each of certain periods are specified, the causal effect on option price at one or more other periods can be determined.

These assumptions hinge on the nature of the information process in a world of uncertainty. Implicit in these assumptions is the inference that new information which comes into the market cannot always be evaluated precisely. Sometimes the stock price change caused by the new information will be quite large, which will set forces in motion to produce a reaction on the price of the option. In other cases, the immediate stock price change will not fully discount the information, and an impetus will be created to move the option price again.

There are four possible sources of friction in the market place, any one of which could affect the processing of information. First, transfer of financial capital among alternative forms of investment is far from costless. Transaction costs may easily exceed returns over short periods of time. Second, information is not costless nor available instantly. Complete company reports are only issued annually in many companies. Furthermore, the life of options is limited by the maturity date. Third, unrealized anticipations determine the structure of option value. Finally, the time horizons of option investors are not too long. Tax rates are markedly higher on short-term gains (or ordinary income) than on long-term capital gains.

The Fundamental Dynamic Equation

Based on these assumptions, it is postulated that the price of an option in equation (2.2) takes the following form:

$$y(t) = \sum_{s=-b_1}^{b_2} \beta_s x_f(t - s) + \varepsilon(t), \tag{2.14a}$$

where $y(t)$, $x_f(t)$ are random variables; $y(t)$ is the option value over all traders in the market; $x_f(t)$ represents either one of the two focus values for the market; β_s is an unknown lag function for periods $s = -b_1, \ldots, b_2$; and $\varepsilon(t)$ is an error term assumed normal with constant variance. Taking expected values on both sides of equation (2.14a), one obtains the expected value of an option given market expectations as to stock price:

$$E[y(t)|x_e] = \sum_{s=-b_1}^{b_2} \beta_s x_f(t-s). \tag{2.14b}$$

Equation (2.14) will be termed the fundamental dynamic equation. It states that, on the average, the option price at time t is a weighted sum of past and future focus values. The lag function β_s represents weights applied in forming stock price expectations at various periods in the past and future.

The basic idea underlying this model can be illustrated in Figure 4, which is a combination of Figures 1 and 3. In order to discuss the model conveniently, ignore for the moment the focus low and consider a given period of time t. Now, investor confidence in the future is reflected in the distance d between the present stock price x_* and the focus high x_h. For example, if investors felt certain that the current stock price would prevail next period, then $x_* = x_h$ with $PS = 0$, so that $x_e(t+1) = x(t)$, implying that the expected option value given these expectations is $E[y(t+1) \mid x_e] = y(t)$. Now the greater investor uncertainty about the future, the greater the distance d. If investors turn their attention to the higher stock price x_h, the corresponding value of Φ will also always be higher. This implies that investors move to a higher ascendency curve. All other things being equal, this implies a larger expected option value to compensate for the increased uncertainty, so that $E[y(t+1) \mid x_e] = \beta x_h$. A similar argument can be given for the focus low to obtain a positive relationship between the focus low and the expected value of an option.

An obvious difficulty with this simple explanation is that it is unrealistic to assume that the value of an option is influenced only by expectations formed at period t. It seems reasonable to assume that the effect of stock expectations on option value depends on the length of different investor horizon periods. Because expectations are subject to change from period to period, it is sensible to generalize the analysis in terms of a dynamic relation over time. This results in the form of equation (2.14).[9]

The Behavioral Dynamic Equation

The expected value of an option to investors who have certain assumed expectations as to stock prices has now been developed. It is not

9. Note that the potential surprise curve is drawn in Figure 4 with the lower extreme reaching a maximum at $x = 0$. This was done intentionally to be consistent with current option theory. Thus, as long as the stock does not reach a price of zero, this theory implies that the option is always worth something to an investor.

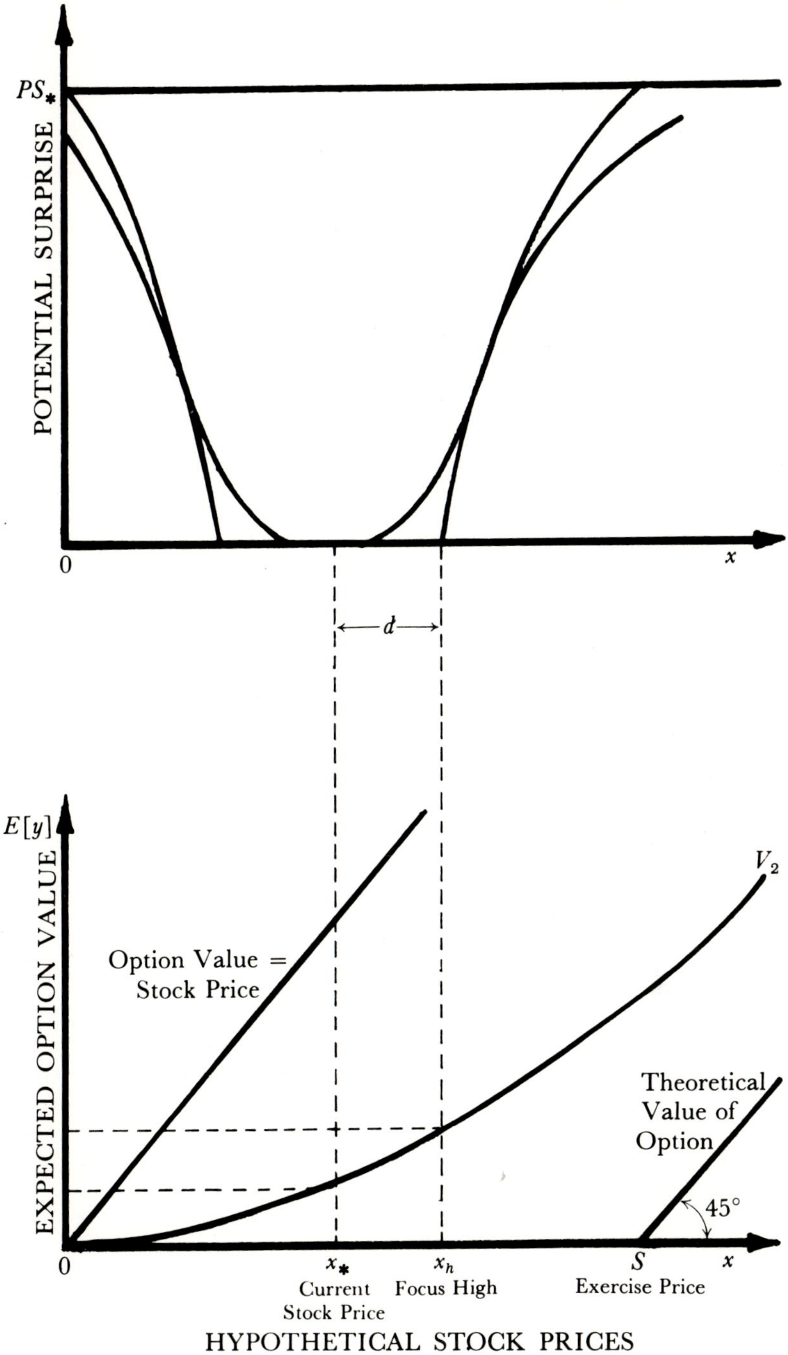

Fig. 4 Dynamic expectations hypothesis

generally true, though, that investors would be willing to pay a price for the option exactly equal to the expected value based on expectations alone. For example, any number of institutional or market factors could make an investor willing to pay something more or less for an option. An extension of (2.14) to allow for additional variables will now be considered.

It will be assumed that factors other than expectations alone influence the value of an option. Although all the additional factors that affect option value are not known, it is assumed that there exists a finite number of them $[z_1(t), \ldots, z_m(t)]$ and a function g such that the value of an option to investors can be determined exactly by

$$y(t) = E[y(t)|x_e] + g[z_1(t), \ldots, z_m(t)]. \tag{2.15}$$

It may not be true that all the factors are capable of being observed; but if they could be observed, one could in principle determine the value of an option exactly.

Suppose that the variables $[z_1(t), \ldots, z_n(t)]$, $n \leqq m$, do a reasonable job of explaining y so that (2.15) becomes

$$\begin{aligned} y(t) = E[y(t)|x_e] &+ g[z_1(t), \ldots, z_n(t)] \\ &+ h[z_{n+1}(t), \ldots, z_m(t)]. \end{aligned} \tag{2.16}$$

Suppose further that the term $h[z_{n+1}(t), \ldots, z_m(t)]$ acts as a normally distributed random variable with constant variance. Under these conditions, and recalling assumptions A1 to A4, it is hypothesized that the value of an option can be modeled as

$$y(t) = \sum_{s=-b_1}^{b_2} \beta_s x_f(t-s) + \sum_{k=1}^{n} \sum_{s=-c_{1k}}^{c_{2,k}} \psi_{ks} z_{ks}(t-s) + \varepsilon(t), \tag{2.17}$$

where $z_1(t), \ldots, z_n(t)$ represent n other factors; $y(t)$, $x_f(t)$, and $z_k(t)$ denote random variables; β_s and ψ_{ks} are unknown lag functions; $-b_1$, b_2, $-c_{1k}$, and c_{2k} identify the dynamic structure of each variable; and $\varepsilon(t)$ is normal with constant variance. Equation (2.17) will be termed the behavioral dynamic equation. It states that option price is a weighted sum of focus values, but that n additional market factors affect expectation formation in the past and future. The lag function ψ_{ks} represents the extent of their influence at various periods in the past and future.

Purposes of This Investigation

Given equations (2.14) and (2.17), the remainder of this book will be directed to identifying and estimating the unknown lag functions β_s, ψ_{ks}.

Briefly outlined, the purposes of this investigation are the following: (1) to use recent statistical methods to develop testable equations for (2.14) and (2.17); (2) to test alternative expectations hypotheses; (3) to test different option price determinant hypotheses; and (4) to present empirical evidence of the actual dynamic behavior of option prices.

3

STATISTICAL CONSIDERATIONS

Introduction

There are certain fundamental concepts which are basic for a complete understanding of the material to follow in Chapters 5 and 6. This chapter will define and discuss these concepts. In particular, the notions of stationary random functions, autocorrelation functions, cross correlation functions, and white noise are developed. A discussion of dynamic models follows these definitions. The procedure of Box and Jenkins (1970) will be principally considered here, and a description of each phase of their iterative modeling process is given.

Random Functions

A function $\xi(t)$, $t \in T = \{\ldots, -1, 0, 1, \ldots\}$, whose values are random will be called a random function. (T is taken as the set of all integers.) Although in analyzing a "time series" one can regard it as a realization of a "stochastic process," both terms will be regarded as synonomous with the term random function. Subscripts will be used when it is necessary to distinguish a random function $\xi_x(t)$ from a random function $\xi_y(t)$.

Autocovariance Functions

The autocovariance function of a random function $\xi(t)$ is defined as

$$\gamma_{(t_1 t_2)}[\xi(t)] = E[\xi(t_1)\xi(t_2)] - E[\xi(t_1)]E[\xi(t_2)], \tag{3.1}$$

where E is the expected value operator and t_1 and t_2 are any two values which may be taken by t.

Stationary Random Functions

A random function is said to be strictly stationary if its distributional properties are unaffected by a change of time origin. A weaker form of stationarity, termed covariance stationary, only requires that the mean and autocovariance function of a random function be invariant over time. More formally, a random function $\xi(t)$ which satisfies the two conditions,

$$E[\xi(t)] = \mu = \text{a constant} \tag{3.2a}$$

and

$$\gamma_{(t_1t_2)}[\xi(t)] = \gamma_{(t_1-t_2)}[\xi(t)] = \gamma_k[\xi(t)], \tag{3.2b}$$

where

$$\gamma_k[\xi(t)] = E[\xi(t) - \mu)(\xi(t+k) - \mu)]$$

makes the autocovariance function a function of $k = t_1 - t_2$ alone and not of t. This is referred to as a covariance stationary function or just a stationary function. With the additional assumption of normality for $\xi(t)$, covariance stationary implies strict stationarity.

Autocorrelation Functions

The autocorrelation function of a stationary random function $\xi(t)$ is defined as

$$\rho_k[\xi(t)] = \frac{\gamma_k[\xi(t)]}{\gamma_0[\xi(t)]} \qquad k = 0, \pm 1, \pm 2, \ldots, \tag{3.3}$$

where $-1 \leqq \rho_k \leqq 1$ with ρ_k being symmetric about the origin. It is therefore necessary only to display the region where $k \geqq 0$.

Estimation of Autocorrelation Functions

The true autocorrelation function in (3.3) describes a conceptual random function. In practice only a finite number of N observations $y(1), y(2), \ldots, y(N)$ are available from which to estimate the autocorrelations. The most frequently used estimate is

$$r_k[y(t)] = \frac{c_k[y(t)]}{c_0[y(t)]} \qquad k = 0, \pm 1, \pm 2, \ldots, \tag{3.4}$$

where if $\bar{y}$ is the sample mean of the series $y(t)$, then an estimate of the autocovariance function is given by

$$(3.5)\quad c_k[y(t)] = \frac{1}{N}\sum_{t=1}^{N-k}[y(t) - \bar{y}][y(t+k) - \bar{y}] \qquad k = 0, \pm 1, \pm 2, \ldots .$$

Cross Covariance Functions

The cross covariance function between two stationary random functions $\xi_x(t)$ and $\xi_y(t)$ with means μ_x and μ_y respectively is

$$(3.6)\qquad \gamma_k[\xi_x(t);\, \xi_y(t)] = E[\xi_x(t) - \mu_x)(\xi_y(t+k) - \mu_y)],$$

where $k = 0, \pm 1, \pm 2, \ldots$. In general, $\gamma_k[\xi_x(t);\, \xi_y(t)]$ will not be the same as $\gamma_k[\xi_y(t);\, \xi_x(t)]$. However, since $\gamma_k[\xi_x(t);\, \xi_y(t)] = \gamma_{-k}[\xi_y(t);\, \xi_x(t)]$, it is common to define only one function for $k = 0, \pm 1, \pm 2, \ldots$, as in equation (3.6).

Cross Correlation Functions

A pair of random functions denoted by $(\xi_x(t), \xi_y(t))$ will be termed a bivariate random function. The cross correlation function of a bivariate random function, with each random function $\xi_x(t)$, $\xi_y(t)$ stationary, is defined as

$$(3.7)\qquad \rho_k[\xi_x(t);\, \xi_y(t)] = \frac{\gamma_k[\xi_x(t);\, \xi_y(t)]}{\sqrt{\gamma_0[\xi_x(t)]}\sqrt{\gamma_0[\xi_y(t)]}},$$

where $k = 0, \pm 1, \pm 2, \ldots$, and $-1 \leqq \rho_k[\xi_x(t);\, \xi_y(t)] \leqq 1$, but $\rho_k[\xi_x(t);\, \xi_y(t)]$ is not symmetric about the origin.

Estimation of Cross Correlation Functions

Given N pairs of observations $(x(1), y(1)), (x(2), y(2)), \ldots, (x(N), y(N))$, an estimate of the cross correlation function between $x(t)$ and $y(t)$ is provided by

$$(3.8)\quad r_k[x(t);\, y(t)] = \frac{c_k[x(t);\, y(t)]}{\sqrt{c_0[x(t)]}\sqrt{c_0[y(t)]}} \qquad k = 0, \pm 1, \pm 2, \ldots,$$

where if $\bar{x}, \bar{y}$ are the sample means for each of the series $x(t), y(t)$, then an estimate of the cross covariance function is

$$(3.9)\qquad c_k[x(t); y(t)] = \frac{1}{N} \sum_{t=1}^{N-k} [x(t) - \bar{x}][y(t+k) - \bar{y}] \quad \text{when } k = 0, 1, 2, \ldots$$

$$= \frac{1}{N} \sum_{t=1}^{N-k} [y(t) - \bar{y}][x(t-k) - \bar{x}] \quad \text{when } k = 0, -1, -2, \ldots.$$

White Noise

A random sequence $\{\varepsilon(t)\}$; $t \in T = \{\ldots, -1, 0, 1, \ldots\}$ with mean

$$(3.10a)\qquad E[\varepsilon(t)] = 0,$$

autocovariance function

$$(3.10b)\qquad \gamma_k[\varepsilon(t)] = E[\varepsilon(t)\varepsilon(t+k)] = \begin{cases} \sigma^2 & \text{for } k = 0 \\ 0 & \text{otherwise,} \end{cases}$$

and autocorrelation function

$$(3.10c)\qquad \rho_k[\varepsilon(t)] = \frac{\gamma_k[\varepsilon(t)]}{\gamma_0[\varepsilon(t)]} = \begin{cases} 1 & \text{for } k = 0 \\ 0 & \text{otherwise} \end{cases}$$

will be termed white noise. This indicates that the random sequence $\varepsilon(t)$ is independent, and is normally distributed with zero mean and constant variance.

Dynamic Models

A general dynamic model in discrete time with additive disturbances is an equation of the form

$$(3.11)\qquad y(t) = \sum_{k=-\infty}^{\infty} g_k x(t-k) + \varepsilon(t)$$

where $x(t), y(t)$ denote deviations from expected values and are in principle observable, $\varepsilon(t)$ is an unobservable white noise series, and g_k is an unknown function for log k.[1] It will always be assumed that the series under consideration are covariance stationary and normally distributed. Values of g_k for positive s apply to past, or lagged, values of x and are referred to as coefficients for "positive lags." Similarly, values of g_k for negative s are coefficients for "negative lags" or future values of x.

The distinguishing features of (3.11) for practical implementation are that (1) it contains unobservable future observations, and (2) it contains an infinite number of parameters. Thus, as it stands, (3.11) is not operational and cannot be estimated.

To alleviate the first problem, most applications of dynamic models assume $g_k = 0$ for all $k < 0$. Then (3.11) simplifies to the dynamic model

$$y(t) = \sum_{k=0}^{\infty} g_k x(t - k) + \varepsilon(t). \tag{3.12a}$$

In econometrics, equation (3.12a) is often referred to as a distributed lag model, and g_k is called the lag function. In engineering contexts, g_k would be referred to as the transfer function of the system. Later discussions will employ extensively the backward shift operator B, which is defined by $Bx(t) = x(t - 1)$, so that for any k, $B^k x(t) = x(t - k)$. Letting $g(B) = \sum_{k=0}^{\infty} g_k B^k$, one can rewrite (3.12a) as

$$y(t) = g(B)x(t) + \varepsilon(t). \tag{3.12b}$$

Given finitely many observations, estimation of the infinite sequence of unknown parameters $g(B)$ is not well defined. It is necessary to impose prior constraints on the form of $g(B)$ to obtain a finite parameter scheme. Then least squares principles can be used to produce unbiased and consistent estimates of the parameters $g(B)$. An efficient method has been proposed independently by Jorgenson (1966) and Box and Jenkins (1970). Their suggestion is to approximate the operator $g(B)$ in (3.12b) by a rational lag function represented by the ratio $\beta(B)/\alpha(B)$ of two finite degree polynomials:

$$\beta(B) = \beta_0 + \beta_1 B + \cdots + \beta_b B^b \tag{3.13a}$$

and

$$\alpha(B) = 1 - \alpha_1 B - \cdots - \alpha_a B^a. \tag{3.13b}$$

1. For expositional ease, the models to follow are concerned with only two variables. Extensions to include several variables create no essential complications. [In this regard, see the section on behavioral dynamic equations in Chapter 6.]

Then equation (3.12) becomes

$$y(t) = \frac{\beta(B)}{\alpha(B)} x(t) + \varepsilon(t), \tag{3.14a}$$

which is equivalent to

$$\begin{aligned} y(t) &= \alpha_1 y(t-1) + \alpha_2 y(t-2) + \cdots + \alpha_a y(t-a) \\ &\quad + \beta_0 x(t) - \beta_1 x(t-1) - \cdots - \beta_b x(t-b) + \varepsilon(t). \end{aligned} \tag{3.14b}$$

Note that as an approximation scheme to the underlying infinite structure, the rational lag procedure tries to accomplish two objectives: (1) to approximate the true lag coefficients closely, and (2) to do so with as few parameters as possible while keeping the estimation scheme relatively simple. An arbitrarily close approximation to $g(B)$ can be achieved with $a = 0$ by choosing sufficiently large values of b. Lagged dependent variables are allowed in (3.14) because an equally close approximation can often be achieved with considerably fewer parameters.

In estimating the parameters of models like (3.14), difficulty arises if the disturbances are not independent. To allow for this, assume that the $\varepsilon(t)$ in (3.14) can be characterized by the linear process

$$\varepsilon(t) = \sum_{k=0}^{\infty} v_k n(t-k) = v(B)n(t), \tag{3.15}$$

where the $n(t)$ is a white noise series. It is also possible to approximate $v(B)$ by the ratio of two finite operators $(\theta(B))/(\phi(B))$, where

$$\theta(B) = 1 - \theta_1 B - \cdots - \theta_q B^q \tag{3.16a}$$

and

$$\phi(B) = 1 - \phi_1 B - \cdots - \phi_p B^p. \tag{3.16b}$$

Equation (3.15) becomes

$$\varepsilon(t) = \frac{\theta(B)}{\phi(B)} n(t), \tag{3.17a}$$

which is equivalent to

$$\begin{aligned} \varepsilon(t) &= \phi_1 \varepsilon(t-1) + \phi_2 \varepsilon(t-2) + \cdots + \phi_p \varepsilon(t-p) \\ &\quad + n(t) - \theta_1 n(t-1) - \cdots - \theta_q n(t-q). \end{aligned} \tag{3.17b}$$

Equation (3.17) can be regarded as a generalization of the first order autoregressive model that has received considerable attention as a means of representing correlated errors. Higher order autoregressive terms allow more general representations of the error series.

Coupling (3.17) with (3.14), the dynamic model in (3.12) can be written as

$$y(t) = \frac{\beta(B)}{\alpha(B)} x(t) + \frac{\theta(B)}{\phi(B)} n(t), \tag{3.18}$$

where $x(t), y(t)$ are deviations from expected values; the roots of the polynomials $\alpha(B)$, $\theta(B)$, and $\phi(B)$ lie outside the unit circle; and the residuals $n(t)$ are white noise and independent of the $x(t)$. It is further assumed that the series under consideration are covariance stationary and normally distributed. Equation (3.18) can be easily extended to include several series on the right side of the equation.

A class of models such as (3.18) will be used in this thesis to investigate the models of Chapter 2 empirically. Given the sample series, however, one must be able to determine a particular member of this class to represent the data. Box and Jenkins (1970) suggest an iterative approach of identification, estimation, and diagnostic checking.

Two-Stage Identification

At the identification stage, it is important to have methods which will clearly demonstrate a model appropriate for the data. Because directions of causality are not always clear a priori, the identification methods used should be general enough to detect the existence of feedback situations. A natural tool to consider for identification is the cross correlation function between two series. Simply stated, this function yields a summary measure of the strength of the relationship between two series over different time intervals.

When dealing with financial time series, however, the cross correlation function can be difficult to interpret because each of the series may itself be autocorrelated. Such autocorrelations can inflate the variance of estimated cross correlations. Moreover, most financial time series are nonstationary, and cross correlating such series would not appear to have much value as an identification procedure.

Haugh (1972) has shown that the problem of interpretation is simplified when one cross correlates two white noise series. Under the additional assumption of series independence, cross correlation estimates can be judged individually against a constant standard error of $N^{-1/2}$ where N is the number of sample observations. Therefore, it will be quite easy to interpret cross correlation estimates only in the situation of two independent white noise series.

Based on the above considerations, this book will employ a two-stage procedure of identification developed by Haugh (1972). The basic idea involved is (1) to characterize each original univariate series as white noise, and (2) to identify a joint model for the relationships between the set of white noise series. To accomplish (2), one can calculate the various cross correlation functions for the different white noise series and propose a tentative model for these series based on the cross correlation patterns. These two stages can then be combined to identify a joint model for the original series.

Haugh (1972) thoroughly examines this two-stage procedure from the point of view of asymptotic theory and Monte Carlo sampling. He concludes that model identification is made more tractable because the cross correlation estimates between white noise series (at stage two) are asymptotically independent with constant variance $N^{-1/2}$ under the assumption of series independence.

Stage One

It has been suggested above that it is useful to analyze the two series $x(t)$ and $y(t)$ separately at the first stage of model identification. This amounts to transforming the original series $x(t), y(t)$ to white noise series.[2] The underlying motivation of this approach is similar to the prefiltering in univariate spectral analysis. Such filtering improves the sampling properties of spectral estimates. In our case it will be assumed that each univariate series can be efficiently represented by an autoregressive–moving average model.[3]

Symbolically, one would first efficiently fit the univariate models

$$\varepsilon(t{:}y) = \frac{\phi_y(B)}{\theta_y(B)}\, y(t) \tag{3.19a}$$

and

$$\varepsilon(t{:}x) = \frac{\phi_x(B)}{\theta_x(B)}\, x(t) \tag{3.19b}$$

to the original series $y(t), x(t)$ where $\varepsilon(t{:}y)$, $\varepsilon(t{:}x)$ are the resulting white noise series.

2. Sections on univariate analysis in Chapter 4 will describe the univariate fitting procedure in more detail and provide examples of the transformation.

3. It is further supposed that nonstationary series can be approximately differenced to induce stationarity. A complete discussion is given in Box and Jenkins (1970).

Stage Two

At the second stage of model identification, one considers the estimated cross correlation function $r_k[\varepsilon(t:x); \varepsilon(t:y)]$ in an attempt to identify a relationship between $x(t)$ and $y(t)$. Three different situations may arise:

1. $r_k[\varepsilon(t:x); \varepsilon(t:y)] = 0$ for all k, in which case the two white noise series are independent;

2. $r_k[\varepsilon(t:x); \varepsilon(t:y)]$ is nonzero only for non-negative k. A dynamic model can then be identified by interpreting particular correlation patterns;

3. $r_k[\varepsilon(t:x); \varepsilon(t:y)]$ is nonzero for both positive and negative k.[4] In this case efficient estimation techniques are invalid unless causality can be redefined to be unidirectional as in (2). If case three occurs during data analysis, indicating the presence of a negative lag of order $|-\kappa|$, the convention adopted in this study will be to shift the series $x(t)$ backward $|-\kappa|$ periods.[5] The net effect of such a procedure is to make $r_k[\varepsilon(t:x); \varepsilon(t:y)]$ nonzero only for non-negative k at the expense of losing $|-\kappa|$ observations. If $|-\kappa|$ is small and the number of observations N is large, then the basic dependence structure between $\varepsilon(t:x)$ and $\varepsilon(t:y)$ will essentially be "shifted" in time. Thus, all parameters are "observable" as in case two, and a dynamic model can be identified.[6]

In using dynamic models, the second stage of model identification is complete when the values a and b of (3.14) are chosen as non-negative numbers. The choice of a and b is determined after examination of the sample cross correlation function. To be able to make a reasonable guess at the proper values, it is necessary for a model builder to be familiar with distinguishing features which occur in the true cross correlation function.[7]

4. This situation is commonly referred to in the literature as the presence of feedback between the two series. A special case of (3) occurs when $r_k[\varepsilon(t:x); \varepsilon(t:y)]$ is nonzero only for negative lags k. This case is handled by the same "shifting" procedure discussed below in the text.

5. The "shifting" procedure is adopted because the main intention of this thesis is to examine the behavior of $y(t)$ in relation to the variable(s) $x(t)$ as in equations (2.14) and (2.17).

6. Similar procedures have been utilized by Sims (1972) and Sargent (1972) to estimate coefficients on future values of the independent variable. They regress y on past and future values of x within the context of two-sided distributed lag functions to test the "expectations hypothesis" of the term structure of interest rates.

7. Various patterns that commonly occur in practice are presented in Box and Jenkins (1970).

Completing Identification

An identified relationship between two white noise series $\varepsilon(t{:}x)$, $\varepsilon(t{:}y)$ can be written as

$$\varepsilon(t{:}y) = \frac{\beta(B)}{\alpha(B)}\,\varepsilon(t{:}x) + \frac{\theta(B)}{\phi(B)}\,n(t). \tag{3.20}$$

Substituting the two univariate models of (3.19) into (3.20) gives the identified model in terms of the original series:[8]

$$y(t) = \frac{\beta(B)\phi_x(B)\theta_y(B)}{\alpha(B)\theta_x(B)\phi_y(B)}\,x(t) + \frac{\theta(B)\theta_y(B)}{\phi(B)\phi_y(B)}\,n(t). \tag{3.21}$$

Parameter Estimates

Having identified one or more tentative models, it is necessary to obtain efficient estimates of the parameters. Assume that the disturbances $n(t)$ are normally distributed. Box and Jenkins (1970) show that under this assumption the maximum likelihood estimates (MLE) of the parameters in (3.21),

$$\alpha_1, \ldots, \alpha_a;\ \beta_0, \ldots, \beta_b;\ \phi_1, \ldots, \phi_p;\ \theta_1, \ldots, \theta_q;$$

$$\phi_{x1}, \ldots, \phi_{xp};\ \theta_{x1}, \ldots, \theta_{xq};\ \phi_{y1}, \ldots, \phi_{yp};\ \theta_{y1}, \ldots, \theta_{yq},$$

are approximately the values that minimize the sum of squares function

$$\sum_{t=1}^{N} [n(t)]^2 = \sum_{t=1}^{N} [y(t) - \hat{y}(t)]^2, \tag{3.22}$$

where $\hat{y}(t)$ is the estimated value of $y(t)$ from an approximately identified model. That is, one has a set of observations and an identified model that supposedly generated these observations. Prior to being generated, the observations were random variables to be drawn from a distribution defined by the particular form of the model and its unknown parameters. Now, having the observations in hand, what values of the parameters are likely to have given rise to these observations?

The procedure recommended by Box and Jenkins for computation of the estimates of the model parameters is to search the sum of squares

8. It is difficult to identify a suitable error model prior to estimation because the errors $\varepsilon(t)$, unlike the $x(t)$, are unobservable. In most instances it is easier to fit an identified model first and assume the error term is white noise, and then examine the residuals for autocorrelations. Although this is the procedure adopted here, the discussion will proceed as if a model for the error term has also been identified.

surface at various values of the parameters until a minimum is found.[9] Box and Jenkins show that as the sample size increases, the estimates calculated by minimizing (3.22) converge to the maximum likelihood estimates.[10]

Preliminary Estimates

Efficient estimation is only possible assuming the model form a, b is known and initial starting values are available that are reasonably close to the values which produce a minimum in (3.22). Initial estimates of an identified model are obtained from a system of linear equations.

To illustrate this, let us consider an appropriately identified model between the two white noise series $\varepsilon(t:x) = x(t)$ and $\varepsilon(t:y) = y(t)$:

$$\varepsilon(t:y) = g(B)\varepsilon(t:x) + \varepsilon(t). \tag{3.23}$$

On multiplying both sides by $\varepsilon(t:x)$ and taking expectations, (3.23) becomes

$$\gamma_k[\varepsilon(t:x);\varepsilon(t:y)] = g_k\gamma_0[\varepsilon(t:x);\varepsilon(t:x)] \tag{3.24}$$

so that

$$g_k = \frac{\gamma_k[\varepsilon(t:x);\varepsilon(t:y)]}{\gamma_0[\varepsilon(t:x)]}, \tag{3.25}$$

or, in terms of cross correlations,

$$g_k = \frac{\rho_k[\varepsilon(t:x);\varepsilon(t:y)]\sqrt{\rho_0[\varepsilon(t:y)]}}{\sqrt{\rho_0[\varepsilon(t:x)]}}. \tag{3.26}$$

9. Dynamic models such as (3.18) are by definition nonlinear, and iterative methods must be employed to minimize (3.22). A method developed by Marquant (1963) appears suitable and will be used in this volume. Marquant's method represents a compromise between the linearization method of Taylor's series and the steepest descent method by combining the best features of both, while avoiding their serious limitations. The algorithm will behave well when the sum of squares (3.22) considered as a function of its unknown parameter value estimates is a quadratic function in the unknown parameters.

10. It is important to note the effect on estimation of the shifting convention adopted in the section on two-stage identification. This shifting procedure formally leads one to consider the joint density of the first $(n - 1)$ observations conditional on all n observations of the independent variable x, plus the nth observation of the dependent variable y. This is unlike the distribution of all n observations conditional only on all observations of x. Consequently, the various sampling distributions, on which later statistical inferences are based, could be altered.

In practice, estimates of the cross correlations can be substituted into (3.26) to provide estimates of g_k. The weights g_k are referred to as the response function. They supply starting values for a series of equations:

$$(3.27\text{a}) \quad g_k = \alpha_1 g_{k-1} + \alpha_2 g_{k-2} + \cdots + \alpha_a g_{k-a} + \beta_0 \quad \text{if } k = 0;$$

$$(3.27\text{b}) \quad g_k = \alpha_1 g_{k-1} + \alpha_2 g_{k-2} + \cdots + \alpha_a g_{k-a} - \beta_s \quad \text{if } k = 1, \ldots, b;$$

$$(3.27\text{c}) \quad g_k = \alpha_1 g_{k-1} + \alpha_2 g_{k-2} + \cdots + \alpha_a g_{k-a} \quad \text{if } k > b.$$

The solution of these equations supplies initial parameter estimates for the lag operators $\alpha(B)$, $\beta(B)$.[11] It should be emphasized that estimates of g_k given by (3.26) for sample cross correlations are necessarily inefficient. They are only employed because (1) they are easily computed, and (2) they can indicate a model form to be fitted by efficient algorithms.

Diagnostic Checks

In order to test the adequacy of the fitted model, several diagnostic statistics can be calculated from the sequentially observed residuals. It is the purpose of these statistics to uncover systematic lack of fit in the model and point the way for modification.

Autocorrelation Checks

The occurrence of marked patterns of the autocorrelation function $r_k[n(t)]$ of the residuals $n(t)$ suggests inadequacy of the error term in (3.18). Examination of the autocorrelation patterns of $r_k[n(t)]$ can sometimes indicate directions for model modification. For small k, though, comparison of estimated autocorrelation in each with a constant standard error could greatly underestimate its significance. Pierce (1968) contributes a helpful overall check that takes account of the distributional effects of fitting in the quantity

$$(3.28) \qquad Q = N \sum_{k=1}^{K} r_k^2[n(t)],$$

which is approximately chi-square distributed with $(K - p - q)$ degrees of freedom for N residuals if the fitted form of the model is adequate.

Cross Correlation Checks

Pierce (1968) also demonstrates that a marked pattern of nonzero sample cross correlations $r_k[\varepsilon(t{:}x); n(t)]$ between the transformed series

11. A complete discussion on the computation of initial parameter estimates is given in Box and Jenkins (1970).

$\varepsilon(t:x)$ and the residuals $n(t)$ suggests inadequacy of the fitted model. An examination of the patterns exhibited by these correlations may indicate how to modify the model. As with the autocorrelations, the distributional effects of using estimated parameters in calculating residuals are confined to low order k. Pierce found that for a correctly specified model the quantities

$$S(+\text{lag}) = N \sum_{k=0}^{K} r_k^2[\varepsilon(t:x); n(t)] \tag{3.29a}$$

and

$$S(-\text{lag}) = N \sum_{k=-K}^{-1} r_k^2[\varepsilon(t:x); n(t)] \tag{3.29b}$$

should be approximately distributed as chi-square, with $(K - r - s)$ and $(K + 1)$ degrees of freedom respectively.

4
DESCRIPTION OF THE DATA AND HYPOTHESES

Types of Options

There are at least five types of common stock options: call options, stock rights, employee options, convertible bonds, and warrants. Basically, they all enable the holder to buy common stock for a given price within a given period of time.

A call is issued by an individual or organization. The standard call contract is negotiable. Calls are customarily written for 30, 60, or 90 days, six months, or one year. Rights are issued by a corporation and usually last for three months at most. Employee options refer to those offered only to employees of a company. They are nonnegotiable instruments which may be exercised only upon certain conditions of employment. Employee options are usually exercisable up to five years but usually become worthless if the owner leaves the company. Convertible securities are issued by the corporation from treasury or authorized stock. These options are nondetachable. Conversion occurs when holders decide to ask for the stock they are entitled to receive in exchange for their convertible security. Convertible bonds are usually exercisable for more than five years. Warrants are a part of a company's capitalization, but they pay no dividends and have no vote nor claim to earnings. In short, they represent solely a privilege to buy shares of common stock. Warrants are usually exercisable for five to ten years. They are typically transferable, many being listed on the major stock exchanges.

The empirical portion of this study will be concerned with *warrants*. Warrants are marketable within a reasonably long option period and are less complicated than convertibles. More important, an analysis of warrants is directly applicable to any kind of option. For example, assume one holds ABC Company $3\frac{7}{8}$ percent 1990 convertible bonds with a purchase value of $800 that are convertible into 20 shares of common stock. If the recent market price of the bond was $1,000, then the conversion privilege is selling for \$200. One could consider the convertible bond to be equal to a bond worth \$800 plus 20 "warrants" worth \$200 or \$10 each. The exercise price for the 20 "warrants" is \$800/20 = \$40 because the bond must be surrendered if the "warrant" is to be exercised.

This chapter discusses the warrants sampled, the particular data series selected, and the sources of data. Each hypothesis to be tested is based on financial theory. Finally, a procedure for transforming each series to white noise is developed. Examples of the method are provided.

The Companies Selected

The data in this study are principally monthly. Only warrants having at least 30 observations were selected. Excluded from consideration was the special class of warrants issued by real estate, investment trust, or holding companies. Also excluded were warrants with the following complications: (1) a company privilege to reduce the exercise price for temporary periods of time; (2) a call privilege enabling the company to redeem the warrants before maturity; and (3) a company privilege to extend the exercise period. This study is further restricted to actively traded securities. Warrants traded over-the-counter are eliminated due to data inconsistencies. These markets report less accurate information when compared with listed markets.

The population consists of all other warrants trading on the New York Stock Exchange (NYSE) and the American Stock Exchange (ASE) on December 31, 1972. The particular warrants selected are shown in Table 1. Time periods vary from warrant to warrant, but in general they run from January 1, 1962, to September 30, 1973, with the final date the same for all warrants. The specific starting date is dependent upon when the warrant began trading on one of the major exchanges after January 1, 1962. In total there are 35 warrants being studied, 5 currently listed on the NYSE and 30 currently listed on the ASE. There are anywhere from 32 to 141 monthly observations per warrant, with an average of approximately 67 observations per warrant.

The plan of this book is to use all 35 warrants to investigate alternate hypotheses of the fundamental dynamic equation in Chapter 2, using two-stage identification. Because extensive machine computations are required to construct dynamic models, it has been necessary to consider for estimation and final model fitting only a sample of the total population. Eight warrants were chosen based on the following criteria:

First, warrants were selected from both the NYSE and the ASE. Investors may view warrants listed on the NYSE to be of higher quality than those listed on the ASE. To the extent that this is true, warrants traded on the NYSE may exhibit different characteristics than ASE warrants. The behavioral traits of the participants on the different

TABLE 1
THE OPTION POPULATION

WARRANT	MONTHLY OBSERVATIONS	PERIOD STUDIED
NYSE		
American Tel & Tel	39	July 1970 – September 1973
Avco	55	March 1969 – September 1973
Gulf & Western	68	February 1968 – September 1973
Northwest	47	November 1969 – September 1973
Williams Cos.	33	January 1971 – September 1973
ASE		
Allegheny Airlines (1987)	75	July 1967 – September 1973
Allegheny Corporation	141	January 1962 – September 1973
Atlas	141	January 1962 – September 1973
Bluebird	46	December 1969 – September 1973
Braniff	65	May 1968 – September 1973
Brown	37	September 1970 – September 1973
Continental Telephone	41	May 1970 – September 1973
Elgin	50	August 1969 – September 1973
Fibreboard	50	August 1969 – September 1973
Flying Tiger	33	January 1971 – September 1973
Frontier Airlines	72	October 1967 – September 1973
Indian Head	99	July 1965 – September 1973
Kane-Miller	43	March 1970 – September 1973
Leasco	54	April 1969 – September 1973
Lerner	65	May 1968 – September 1973
Loews	58	December 1968 – September 1973
McCrory (1976)	135	July 1962 – September 1973
McCrory (1981)	89	May 1966 – September 1973
National General (1974)	107	November 1964 – September 1973
National General (1978)	59	November 1968 – September 1973
National Industries	58	December 1968 – September 1973
Northern Natural Gas	37	September 1970 – September 1973
P.S.A.	63	July 1968 – September 1973
Tenneco	53	May 1969 – September 1973
Textron	73	September 1967 – September 1973
Trans World Airlines	141	January 1962 – September 1973
Uris	121	September 1963 – September 1973
U.V. Industries	48	October 1969 – September 1973
Ward	56	February 1969 – September 1973
Whittaker	53	May 1969 – September 1973

exchanges may also vary. Second, the companies which issued the eight warrants are among the largest and most important as judged by Fortune 500.[1] As a result the common stocks of these companies are probably members of a similar risk class. Finally, the eight warrants selected each

1. *Fortune* 87 (1973): 220–49.

have about 50 monthly observations. The statistical procedures of Chapter 3 require a reasonably large number of observations. When this requirement is not satisfied, parameter estimates are not as reliable as those based on a large number of observations. A brief synopsis of the eight warrants is given in Table 2.

Types and Sources of Data

The price paid in terms of computer time alone to implement dynamic models is substantially more than that required to implement multiple regression models. As a result it has also been necessary to restrict the set of price determinants. To alleviate this problem somewhat, it was decided to develop hypotheses that have not consistently appeared in the warrant literature. Each will be discussed below.

Prices

The principal determinant of option value as suggested by the fundamental dynamic equation of Chapter 2 is stock price expectations represented by focus values. One should expect that higher (lower) focus values result in higher (lower) warrant values. These expectations are hypothesized to be closely related to the price behavior of the stock rather than fundamental company data such as earnings, dividends, etc. Warrant investors are usually characterized as speculators, and speculators are attracted to price changes.

A quantitative measure of focus values is not clearly defined, but a reasonable proxy might be the actual high and low stock price during a month. These high and low prices represent the actual upper and lower bounds of the stock price during a given month. The observed highs and lows can be considered ex post approximations to the ex ante focus values that actually determine investor behavior but cannot be observed.

An experimental study by Burrell (1950) indirectly lends support to the high and low stock prices as proxies for the focus values. He concludes that the price paid for a stock tends to establish its value in the mind of the buyer. As a result, when the price moves below cost, he is likely to buy more. When the price recovers from a low point, he is inclined to sell without waiting to recover full cost. If the price falls from a high, this theory suggests that the former high will become something of a barrier for an upward movement in the future.

Price Data

Monthly closing prices were collected for each of the warrants in Table 1. Monthly high, low, and closing prices were collected for the

TABLE 2
DESCRIPTIONS OF THE SELECTED COMPANIES

COMPANY	PRINCIPAL BUSINESS	EXCHANGE OF WARRANT	EXCHANGE OF COMMON	CURRENT OPTION PRICE	EXPIRATION DATE	SENIOR SECURITY
Allegheny Airlines (1987)	Largest local air carrier of passengers	ASE	ASE	1.04 at 18	4/1/87	$5\frac{1}{2}\%$ Sub Deb '87
American Telephone & Telegraph	Bell System electronics; about 88% of telephone service in U.S.	NYSE	NYSE	1 at $52	5/15/75	None
Avco	Financial services; aerospace; insurance, subsidiary; films, broadcasting	NYSE	NYSE	1 at $56	11/30/78	$7\frac{1}{2}\%$ Deb '93
Gulf & Western	Diversified industrial and financial enterprises	NYSE: from ASE 9/7/71	NYSE	1.027 at $55	1/31/78	None
Loews	Cigarettes; hotels; motels; theatre chain	ASE	NYSE	1 at $37.50	11/29/80	$6\frac{7}{8}\%$ Deb '93
Northwest	Holding company: Scotch distributor; apparel, boots; tubular steel	NYSE: from ASE 11/17/69	NYSE	1 at $25	3/31/79	$7\frac{1}{2}\%$ Deb '94
Tenneco	Natural gas pipeline; oil and gas explorers; land; shipbuilding	ASE	NYSE	1.07 at $32	4/1/79	6% Deb '79
Trans World Airlines	U.S. and foreign air carriers	ASE	NYSE	1 at $22	12/1/73	$6\frac{1}{2}\%$ Sub Inc. Deb '78

Source: *Standard and Poor's Stock Guide*. New York: Standard and Poor's Corporation, September 1973.

associated common stocks. For comparative purposes these market prices were normalized for each company in relation to the exercise price. Assume that with A warrants plus B dollars one can convert the warrant into C common shares. Let $WP_c(t)$ be the closing warrant price for month t and let $CP_c(t)$, $CP_h(t)$, $CP_l(t)$ be the closing, high, and low stock price for month t. The normalized closing warrant price for month t is

$$Y_c(t) = WP_c(t)/(B/A). \tag{4.1a}$$

The normalized closing, normalized high, and normalized low common price for month t are, respectively,

$$X_c(t) = CP_c(t)/(B/C), \tag{4.1b}$$

$$X_h(t) = CP_h(t)/(B/C), \tag{4.1c}$$

and

$$X_l(t) = CP_l(t)/(B/C). \tag{4.1d}$$

Samuelson (1965a) and others have used exactly the same procedure. After this adjustment all normalized warrants allow an investor to purchase one share of common stock.

A basic practice when using price series is to compensate for the fact that such series will frequently contain trends both in means and in variances. It is a common assumption in economics that the effectiveness of a price change relates not to the extent of the change so much as to the extent of the percentage price change. Moore (1964), for instance, has shown that the variability of simple price changes for a given stock is an increasing function of the price level of the stock.

For these reasons, this study will be concerned with one-period rates of change which are simple transforms of the price series. This transformation is clearly sensible as it will remove or limit the importance of any heterogeneity in variance in the original price series.

The percentage change or one-period return for each warrant may be defined as

$$y_c(t) = [Y_c(t) - Y_c(t-1)]/Y_c(t-1). \tag{4.2a}$$

For the common stock, the percentage change or one-period return is

$$x_c(t) = [D(t) + X_c(t) - X_c(t-1)]/X_c(t-1), \tag{4.2b}$$

where $D(t)$ is the dividend paid in period t. The one-period rate of change for the focus high and the focus low are, respectively,

$$x_h(t) = [X_h(t) - X_h(t-1)]/X_h(t-1) \tag{4.2c}$$

and

$$x_l(t) = [X_l(t) - X_l(t-1)]/X_l(t-1). \tag{4.2d}$$

Although the use of percentage change data tends to lessen the effects of multicollinearity and autocorrelation, there is no reason for supposing that the above transformation is the only relevant one. Two other candidates are (1) relative price changes, and (2) changes in log prices. When considering subtle aspects of the distribution of the price changes, the transformation could be of considerable relevance. For instance, the above transformation might produce a symmetric distribution, whereas logarithmic differences may produce a distribution which is skewed. Given these considerations, the empirical analysis to follow was performed for all three transformations of the price series: relative price changes, changes in log prices, and percentage price changes. Because no significant differences were observed in the three sets of results, only the analysis based on the percentage price changes in (4.2) will be reported.[2]

Volume

Volume is often hypothesized as relevant to price, using the rationale that large volume usually accompanies large price changes. The purpose of a volume variable is to reflect marketability or liquidity in some way. It is likely that volume also reflects institutional interests, in addition to the thickness or thinness of the market. Thinness of the market may affect the effectiveness of speculation in smoothing out random noise in price. One would also expect that frequent revisions of investor expectations would generate an increase in volume because trading implies, to an extent, differing expectations among investors. For example, if most of the revisions were upward during a period, high volume might be associated with greater than expected returns.

Hsu (1973) observed that large price changes quite frequently accompanied jumps in volume. He suggests that jumps in volume may be caused by a piece or pieces of unusually good or bad information. In-

2. For expositional ease, the presentation to follow will use the terms interchangeably: *series*, *price*, and *price changes*, prefixed with the words *warrant*, *common*, *focus high*, and *focus low*.

vestors may then change their expectations about future prices and rush to the market to "irrationally" buy or sell securities at certain prices.

Volume Data

Monthly volume figures were collected in Table 2 for each of the warrants and their associated stocks. The warrant volume series for month t will be denoted by $z_1(t)$, while the volume series of the stock for month t is denoted by $z_2(t)$. No differencing was applied to the volume series because the mechanism generating trade volume is based on a concept of flow rather than level.

Volatility

Volatility (or capital risk) and price changes are thought to be positively related; the greater the variance of price, the greater the expected value of the security. The idea is simply that if a security fluctuates a great deal in price about a fixed level, one should expect such securities to show above average rates of return. Current theory in the fields of investment and finance are directed along the lines that the market would price assets so that their expected rate of return and risk would clear the market. For example, Merton (1973) shows that the more risky the common stock, the more valuable the warrant. (He is, of course, referring to total risk and not to portfolio risk.) The results of Sprenkle (1961), Kassouf (1965), and others also suggest that the value of a warrant increases with greater stock price variability.

Volatility Data

Volatility figures were collected for each of the eight warrants in Table 2. Capital risk or volatility will be defined to be the standard deviation of daily returns for nonoverlapping monthly periods. More specifically, let $Y_d(t)$ be the normalized closing price of a warrant for day t, and let $X_d(t)$ be the normalized closing price of its stock for day t. Then the daily return from holding the warrant is

$$(4.3a) \qquad y_d(t) = [Y_d(t) - Y_c(t-1)]/Y_d(t-1),$$

and the daily return from holding the stock is

$$(4.3b) \qquad x_d(t) = [D(t) + X_c(t) - X_c(t-1)]/X_c(t-1),$$

where $D(t)$ is the dividend paid.

The volatility series of the warrant is then the standard deviation of

$y_d(t)$, denoted $z_3(t)$, with the computation performed separately for each nonoverlapping month t. Similarly, the volatility of the stock is the series $z_4(t)$, which represents the standard deviation of daily returns for nonoverlapping months t.

Senior Security

Some options enable the holder to exercise them with either cash or a senior debt security. With this added feature, the effective exercise cost now depends on interest rate levels (in comparison with the coupon rate of the senior security) and is therefore a variable rather than a fixed price.

It is hypothesized that the value of bond usable warrants may be influenced by changes in market interest rates. Given a fixed coupon rate, a decrease in interest rates can not increase the effective exercise cost beyond the fixed exercise price. In general, a lower effective exercise cost results from an increase in market rates. The latter change should increase the value of bond usable warrants to investors.

Van Horne (1969) was the first to recognize the positive effect of higher interest rates on warrant value. Although their results were not statistically significant, Melicher and Rush (1974) observed that warrant investors consider short-term interest rate risk in valuing bond usable warrants.

Senior Security Data

Of the eight warrants in Table 2, six have senior debt securities. The influence of market rates was treated as another exogenous variable.[3] Monthly closing prices were collected for each of the six debt securities. The data correspond to the time period of the warrant. Similar to the previous price series, the data are transformed to allow for trends in means and in variance. Let $SS(t)$ be the closing price of the senior security for month t. The one period rate of change for the senior security is then

$$z_5(t) = [SS(t) - SS(t-1)]/SS(t-1). \tag{4.4}$$

3. All empirical results to follow were also obtained using another treatment of market rates. When significant differences occur, they will be discussed in the text. Exercise prices were adjusted from fixed to variable quantities. This method directly affects the normalized price series. Let $SS(t)$ be the closing price of the senior security for month t and let PAR be its par value. Now if $SS(t)/PAR \geqq 1.0$, then the equations in (4.1) remain unchanged; but for $SS(t)/PAR < 1.0$, the series become $Y_c^*(t) = WP_c(t)/(B/A)(SS(t)/PAR)$; $X_c^*(t) = CP_c(t)/(B/C)(SS(t)/PAR)$ and $X_h^*(t) = CP_h(t)/(B/C)(SS(t)/PAR)$; $X_l^*(t) = CP_l(t)/(B/C)(SS(t)/PAR)$. The one period rates of change in (4.2) then become $y_c^*(t) = [Y_c^*(t) - Y_c^*(t-1)]/Y_c^*(t-1)$; $x_c^*(t) = [X_c^*(t) - X_c^*(t-1)]/X_c^*(t-1)$ and $x_h^*(t) = [X_h^*(t) - X_h^*(t-1)]/X_h^*(t-1)$; $x_l^*(t) = [X_l^*(t) - X_l^*(t-1)]/X_l^*(t-1)$.

Sources of Data

Market values were punched and verified directly from published information. Monthly data came from the *Bank and Quotation Record* and *Standard and Poor's Stock Guide,* while daily quotations came from the *Wall Street Journal* and the *ISL Daily Stock Price Index.* All data have been adjusted for stock splits and stock dividends.

A minor contribution of the present research was collection of a large body of time series data over an extended period for individual warrants on the NYSE and ASE. Previous studies have been primarily concerned with cross sectional data quoted on a few randomly selected dates. Descriptive statistics for each of the data series assembled are provided in Appendix A for the eight warrants in Table 2.

Univariate Series Analysis

In discussing two-stage model identification in the section on two-stage identification, it was assumed that each univariate series could be characterized as white noise. The purpose of this section is to outline a parametric modeling procedure developed by Box and Jenkins (1970).[4] Each series in the previous section about types and sources of data was transformed to white noise by using this procedure.

The methodology of Box and Jenkins describes a procedure for identifying a particular time series model from a class of models, estimating the parameters of that model, and then examining the ability of the fitted model to duplicate the behavior of the given time series data. More specifically, a class of models termed the *autoregressive–moving average class* (ARMA) is postulated to represent a given series. This class of models has been shown to represent most types of series likely to occur in practice. An ARMA random sequence of order p, q, denoted ARMA(p, q), takes the form

$$y(t) = \phi_1 y(t-1) + \phi_2 y(t-2) + \cdots + \phi_p y(t-p) + \varepsilon(t{:}y) - \theta_1\varepsilon(t-1{:}y) - \cdots - \theta_q\epsilon(t-q{:}y), \tag{4.5}$$

4. The reader may be perplexed with reference both here and in Chapter 3 to "Box and Jenkins procedures." In Chapter 3, the method refers to multivariate dynamic models where one desires to relate, for example, a price series to one or more price determinants. This section will review univariate methods where one desires to examine a single series in terms of its current and past values. To distinguish these models the operators $\theta(B)$, $\phi(B)$ are used for univariate models, whereas the operators $\alpha(B)$, $\beta(B)$ are used for multivariate dynamic models. A complete description of both modeling procedures is given in Box and Jenkins (1970).

where $y(t)$ is a given series at period t and $\varepsilon(t{:}y)$ represents the residuals for series y at period t.[5]

By introducing an autoregressive operator of order p,

$$\phi(B) = 1 - \phi_1 B - \phi_2 B^2 - \cdots - \phi_p B^p, \tag{4.6a}$$

and a moving average operator of order q,

$$\theta(B) = 1 - \theta_1 B - \theta_2 B^2 - \cdots - \theta_q B^q, \tag{4.6b}$$

the ARMA(p, q) model may be written economically as

$$y(t) = \frac{\theta(B)}{\phi(B)}\, \varepsilon(t{:}y). \tag{4.7}$$

Given an ARMA(p, q) class of models, the Box–Jenkins procedure requires skilled judgment by the user. The procedure is implemented by an iterative three-stage procedure: (1) identification, (2) parameter estimation, and (3) diagnostic checking.

Model identification consists of choosing the parameters p, q of the ARMA(p, q) class as non-negative integers. The principal tool used to determine p and q is the sample autocorrelation function.[6] The criterion for model selection used in this thesis has been the representation of each series in the most parsimonious form that is consistent with its stochastic structure.

Having identified one or more tentative models, estimates for the parameters $\phi_1, \ldots, \phi_p$; $\theta_1, \ldots, \theta_q$ can be iteratively computed by searching the sum of squares surface for a minimum as discussed in the section on two-stage identification.

The adequacy of the fitted model for the data can be checked by examining the residuals $\varepsilon(t{:}y)$. Any deviation of the observed residuals from that of white noise indicates a lack of fit and must be incorporated into the original model through re-identification. The steps of identification, estimation, and diagnostic checking are repeated until the diagnostic phase indicates that a suitable representation of the data has been found.

5. Univariate Box–Jenkins models will be denoted ARMA(p, q). The autoregressive integrated moving average (ARIMA) model of order (p, d, q) discussed in Box and Jenkins (1970) suggests that homogeneous nonstationary behavior can be represented by a model which specifies that the dth difference of the process to be stationary (with d usually 0, 1, or 2). Here it is assumed that nonstationary series can be approximately differenced, if necessary, to induce stationarity; but notation including the degree of differencing d— will not be used.

6. An extensive discussion of the behavior of the autocorrelation function is given in Box and Jenkins (1970).

Examples of Univariate Analysis

The process of modeling univariate time series discussed in the previous section should be viewed as an attempt to find a transformation that reduces the observed data series to white noise. If one has succeeded in this, then one should expect to find that the residuals have the properties of random numbers. With this in mind, the Box–Jenkins procedure is illustrated in this section for selected price series of Avco Corporation. These examples will serve to explain the method of transformation as it was applied to all companies. Only estimated autocorrelation functions will be presented for the remaining series.[7]

Warrant Series

The estimated autocorrelations of the warrant series $y_c(t)$ for Avco Corporation are shown in Figure 5. To gain some insight as to whether the magnitude of these sample autocorrelations is sufficiently large, consider the hypothesis that $y_c(t)$ is white noise. On the white noise hypothesis, the sample autocorrelations should be approximately normally distributed about zero with standard errors approximately $N^{-1/2} = 0.13$. Durbin (1970) has pointed out that, even if a particular model is appropriate, the autocorrelation function of the residuals from fitting can be markedly different from that of white noise. To allow for this effect, Pierce (1968) has shown that a rough overall test of the residuals can be obtained by referring the Q statistic to a χ^2 table with $(N - p - q)$ degrees of freedom where p and q are the parameters of the ARMA(p, q) model.

Inspection of the two standard error limits in Figure 5 and a rough overall test obtained by referring

$$Q = N \sum_{k=1}^{20} r_k^2[y_c(t)] = 10.0$$

to a χ^2 table with 20 degrees of freedom shows the estimated autocorrelations to be about the magnitude expected on the white noise hypothesis. Accordingly, an adequate model for the data is

$$y_c(t) = \varepsilon(t:y_c) \tag{4.8}$$

with residual variance $\hat{\sigma}^2\varepsilon(t:y_c) = .2178\text{E}–01$ (54df).[8]

7. All data series have been centered about their sample means before application of the univariate analysis.

8. The notation .2178E–01 will be used frequently for the presentation of results in this thesis. It identifies the datum as a real number in exponential form, so that .2178E–01 = .02178.

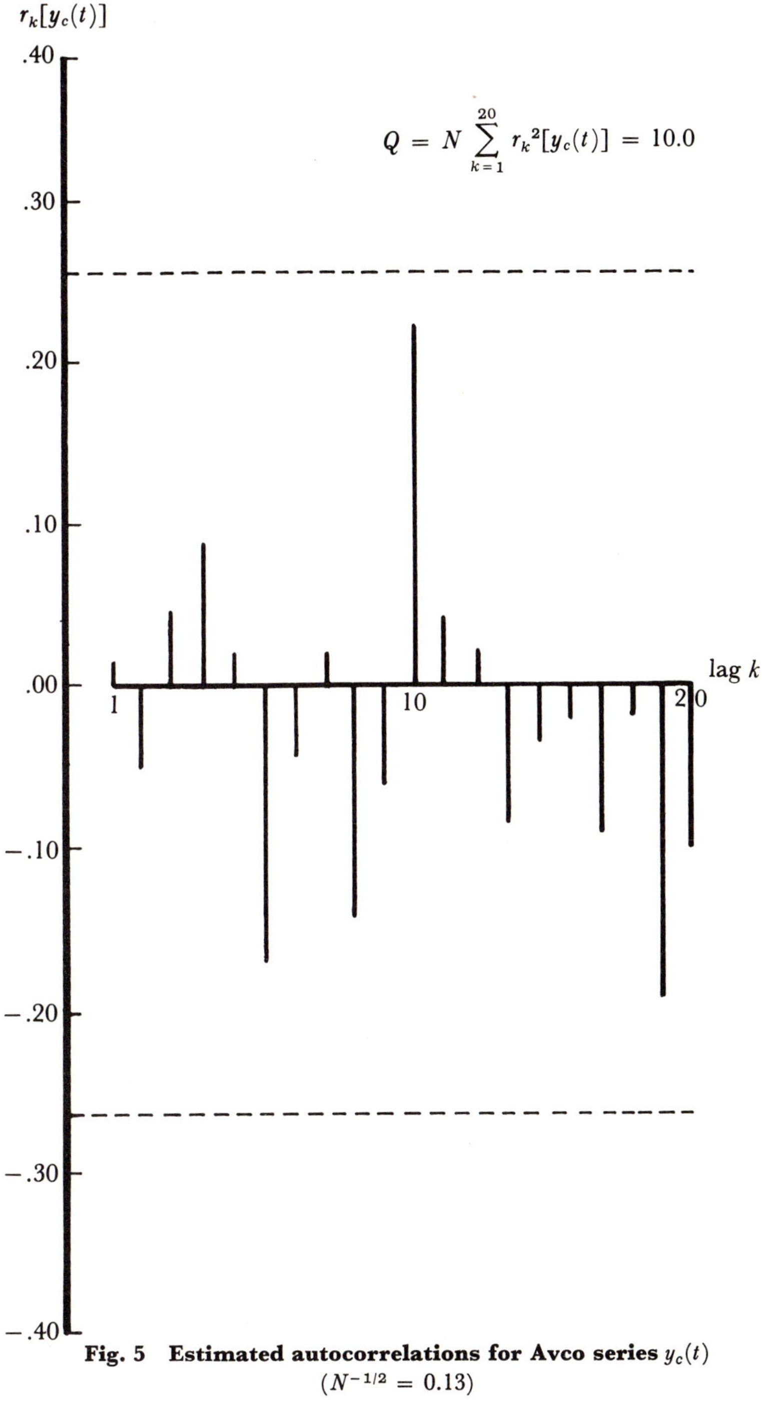

Fig. 5 Estimated autocorrelations for Avco series $y_c(t)$
($N^{-1/2} = 0.13$)

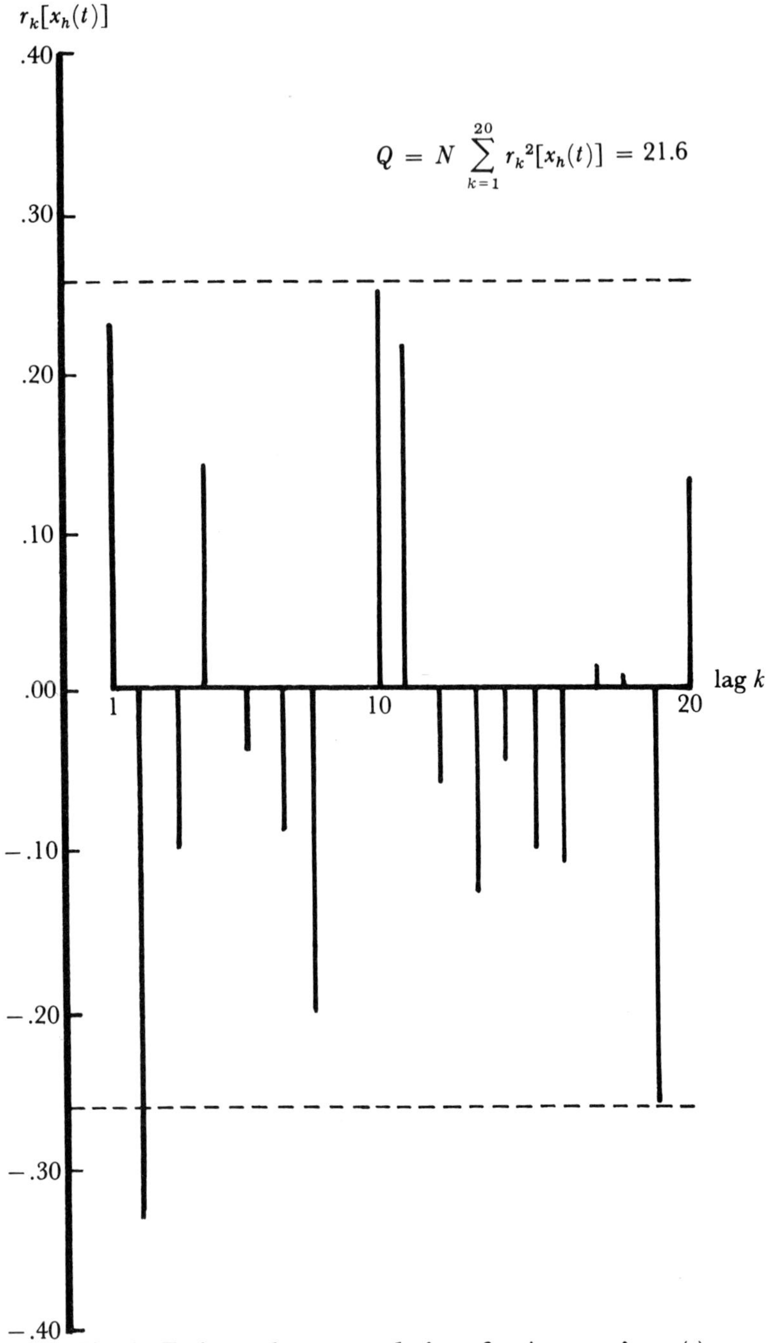

Fig. 6 Estimated autocorrelations for Avco series $x_h(t)$
($N^{-1/2} = 0.13$)

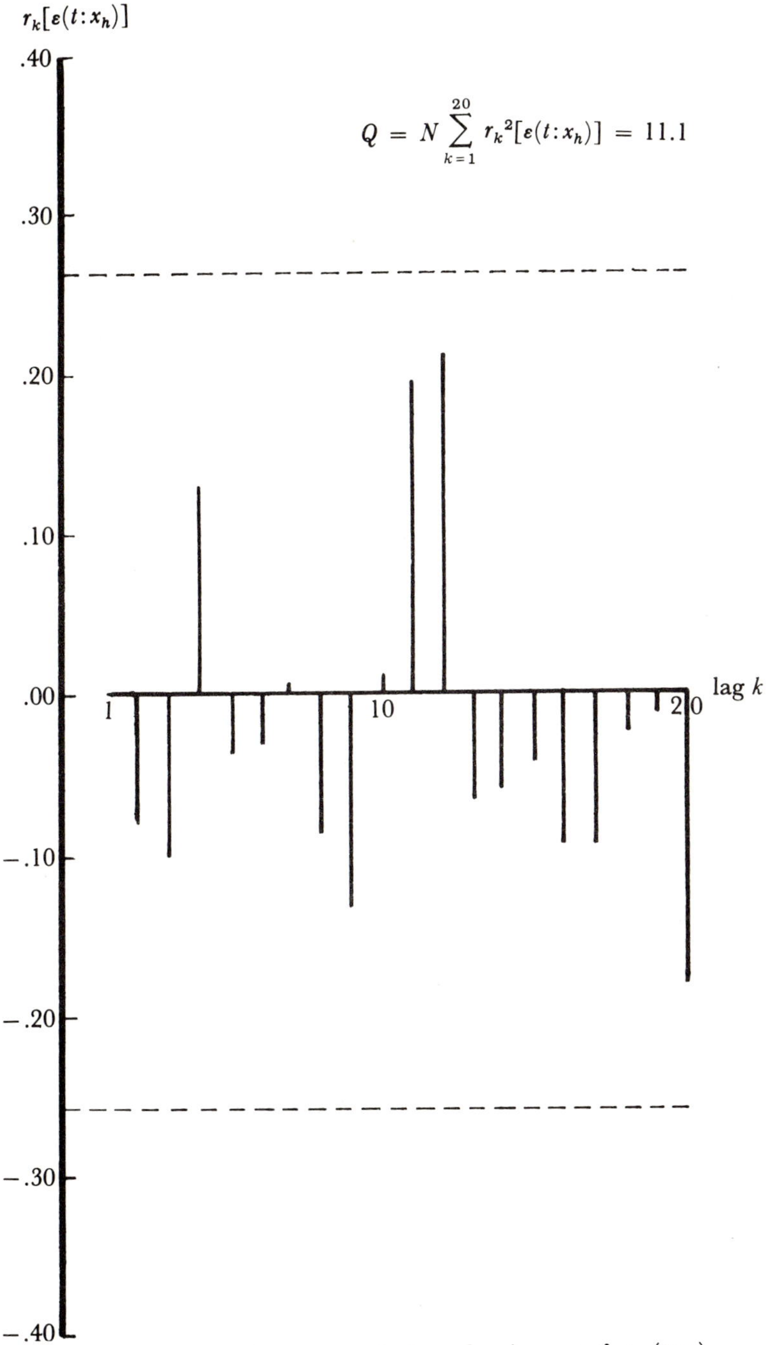

Fig. 7 Estimated autocorrelations for Avco series $\varepsilon(t:x_h)$
($N^{-1/2} = 0.13$)

Focus High Series

The sample autocorrelations of the focus high series $x_h(t)$ for Avco Corporation are shown in Figure 6. The autocorrelations at low lags are moderately large. This is typical of moving average behavior. Accordingly, an adequate model seems to be

$$x_h(t) = \varepsilon(t:x_h) + \underset{(.137)}{.246}\varepsilon(t-1:x_h) - \underset{(.137)}{.219}\varepsilon(t-2:x_h), \tag{4.9}$$

with residual variance $\hat{\sigma}^2\varepsilon(t:x_h) = .1197\text{E–}01$ (52df).

Figure 7 shows the autocorrelation function of the residuals from fitting the model of equation (4.9) to the data. Applying the results of Pierce (1968) one obtains

$$Q = N \sum_{k=1}^{20} r_k{}^2[\varepsilon(t:y_c)] = 11.1.$$

Comparison of this figure with tabulated χ^2 values for 18 degrees of freedom and inspection of Figure 8 yields little evidence of the necessity to employ a more elaborate model.

The Remaining Series

Autocorrelation functions for lags one to ten of the price series y_c, x_c, x_h, x_l for each of the companies sampled are given in Table 3 and in

TABLE 3
ESTIMATED AUTOCORRELATIONS OF THE PRICE SERIES

SERIES	1	2	3	4	5	6	7	8	9	10
74 OBS					ALLEGHENY AIRLINES (1987)					
y_c	.03	−.18	−.10	.10	−.07	−.30	.07	.16	.01	−.04
x_c	−.02	−.01	−.09	−.04	−.05	−.26	.07	−.06	.12	.07
x_h	.22	−.05	.02	−.11	−.13	−.23	−.06	.06	.16	.10
x_l	.21	−.05	−.07	−.18	−.07	−.12	−.12	.03	.16	.17
38 OBS					AMERICAN TELEPHONE & TELEGRAPH					
y_c	.03	−.02	−.03	−.20	−.19	.04	−.24	−.13	.11	−.04
x_c	.08	−.09	.01	−.14	−.07	−.06	−.18	.01	.05	−.08
x_h	−.03	−.03	.07	−.13	.04	−.17	−.20	.18	−.24	.05
x_l	.14	−.02	.10	−.11	−.19	.03	−.04	−.25	.00	−.07
54 OBS					AVCO					
y_c	.02	−.05	.05	.09	.02	−.16	−.03	.01	−.14	−.05
x_c	−.02	−.08	−.03	.02	.11	−.26	.11	−.01	−.25	.07
x_h	.22	−.31	−.09	.15	.00	−.03	.03	−.09	−.18	.00
x_l	.12	−.13	.13	.02	−.10	.05	.07	−.18	−.16	−.01

(continued)

TABLE 3 *Continued*

SERIES	1	2	3	4	5	6	7	8	9	10
67 OBS					GULF & WESTERN					
y_c	.09	.17	.04	.06	.00	.06	.10	−.28	.00	−.05
x_c	.13	.13	−.06	.08	.08	.01	.11	−.26	.00	−.05
x_h	.18	.09	.14	.01	.06	.00	−.02	−.04	−.14	.11
x_l	.18	.03	.14	.13	−.07	.02	.06	−.05	−.19	.16
57 OBS					LOEWS					
y_c	.05	.17	.00	.07	−.15	−.01	−.03	−.08	.08	.07
x_c	.14	.12	.02	.05	−.13	−.05	−.01	−.20	.14	.12
x_h	.21	.17	.08	−.07	−.04	.01	−.16	.01	.14	.06
x_l	.26	−.02	.26	.04	−.27	−.01	.07	−.13	.02	.27
46 OBS					NORTHWEST					
y_c	.01	−.03	.09	.12	.14	.09	.16	.07	−.13	.02
x_c	.07	−.11	−.13	.05	.14	.14	.11	−.03	−.16	−.07
x_h	.19	.04	−.09	.07	.21	.21	.08	−.09	−.05	−.03
x_l	.08	−.05	.00	−.08	.13	.12	.16	.04	−.24	−.08
52 OBS					TENNECO					
y_c	−.15	.16	.09	−.04	−.22	−.08	−.07	−.04	.02	−.06
x_c	−.03	.18	.07	.01	−.15	.03	−.28	−.05	−.10	−.05
x_h	−.06	.18	.14	.03	−.13	−.07	−.05	−.17	−.01	−.23
x_l	.17	.14	.14	−.12	−.09	−.02	−.12	−.19	−.22	.15
140 OBS					TRANS WORLD AIRLINES					
y_c	.00	.00	.11	.14	.13	−.01	.12	.01	.09	−.05
x_c	.04	−.03	.04	.21	.11	.02	.07	.01	.17	−.04
x_h	.05	.10	.15	.11	−.01	.10	.10	.11	.04	−.02
x_l	.18	−.01	.05	.16	.16	.08	.03	.04	.15	.04

Appendix B. In general, the estimated autocorrelations are about the magnitude to be expected under a white noise hypothesis.

Estimated autocorrelations for each of the remaining series z_1, z_2, z_3,

TABLE 4
ESTIMATED AUTOCORRELATIONS OF THE EXOGENOUS SERIES

SERIES	1	2	3	4	5	6	7	8	9	10
75 OBS					ALLEGHENY AIRLINES (1987)					
z_1	.51	.35	.15	.06	−.05	−.05	−.13	−.14	−.15	−.14
z_2	.58	.48	.51	.29	.14	.10	.07	.06	.09	.07
z_3	.11	.02	−.10	−.04	−.10	−.03	−.02	−.09	−.04	.02
z_4	−.05	.05	−.20	−.15	.02	.10	.10	−.26	.07	−.16
z_5	.01	−.11	−.08	.08	.12	−.08	.07	−.24	.06	−.02

(continued)

TABLE 4 *Continued*

SERIES	1	2	3	4	5	6	7	8	9	10
39 OBS					AMERICAN TELEPHONE & TELEGRAPH					
z_1	.01	.01	−.15	−.10	−.05	.22	−.07	−.10	−.10	.04
z_2	.49	.38	.28	.10	.11	.13	−.06	.03	.02	.02
z_3	.31	.33	.18	.10	.17	.23	.20	.09	.09	−.07
z_4	.03	.08	.02	−.07	.16	−.09	−.25	−.05	−.05	.18
55 OBS					AVCO					
z_1	.51	.35	.39	.21	.05	.04	.02	.04	.09	.03
z_2	.41	.23	.10	.00	.02	−.05	.01	−.06	.04	−.13
z_3	.31	.32	.20	.22	.08	.01	.04	−.09	−.08	−.24
z_4	.19	.29	.06	.16	.11	.08	.03	−.10	−.06	−.26
z_5	.11	−.04	.06	−.02	−.20	−.08	.08	−.07	−.12	.06
68 OBS					GULF & WESTERN					
z_1	.47	.17	.13	.00	−.02	−.08	−.12	−.04	−.07	−.03
z_2	.64	.47	.34	.23	.22	.20	.29	.29	.26	.20
z_3	.44	.20	.17	.13	.18	.03	−.07	.03	.14	−.01
z_4	.50	.37	.29	.37	.30	.18	.23	.26	.34	.23
58 OBS					LOEWS					
z_1	.42	.28	.31	.29	.30	.11	−.12	−.07	−.01	−.04
z_2	.43	.38	.29	.23	.25	.04	.03	.04	−.01	.01
z_3	.46	.11	.12	.17	.02	.01	.07	−.02	.04	.07
z_4	.34	.18	.13	.28	.29	.24	.25	.22	.19	.18
z_5	.12	−.10	−.08	.12	−.02	−.03	−.04	−.11	.02	−.01
47 OBS					NORTHWEST					
z_1	.78	.66	.55	.49	.34	.24	.20	.07	.02	−.02
z_2	.39	.23	.32	.36	.20	.01	.25	.11	.07	.10
z_3	.01	.03	.01	.02	.04	.01	.02	.01	.01	.00
z_4	.65	.57	.55	.52	.46	.32	.28	.24	.17	.08
z_5	.10	−.11	−.20	−.02	.26	.00	−.15	−.17	−.09	.06
53 OBS					TENNECO					
z_1	.49	.47	.22	.22	.18	.13	.11	.00	−.06	−.15
z_2	.66	.48	.28	.04	.04	−.10	−.07	−.09	−.14	−.19
z_3	.35	.23	.09	.08	.00	.10	.04	−.01	−.04	.00
z_4	.27	.17	−.08	.12	−.02	.06	−.01	−.08	−.13	−.02
z_5	−.07	.02	−.18	.05	−.09	−.02	.03	−.04	.01	−.03
141 OBS					TRANS WORLD AIRLINES					
z_1	.31	.35	.45	.12	.33	.12	.10	.02	−.11	.07
z_2	.65	.61	.56	.51	.48	.47	.43	.44	.41	.43
z_3	.41	.36	.41	.25	.21	.15	.10	.08	.12	.03
z_4	.41	.36	.28	.24	.25	.15	.09	.04	.11	.08
z_5	.06	.00	−.08	−.02	.14	.04	.02	.06	.05	.06

z_4, z_5 are given in Table 4 for lags one to ten. Sample autocorrelations for the series z_1, z_2 decline exponentially, suggesting that volume can be modeled as ARMA(p, 0) with p no larger than two. This is consistent with the results reported by Granger and Morgenstern (1970). Identification of the volatility series z_3, z_4 indicates a variety of ARMA(p, q) models with p or q no larger than two. Each of the senior security series z_5 has a sample autocorrelation function consistent with the assumption of white noise.

5

DATA ANALYSIS OF THE FUNDAMENTAL DYNAMIC EQUATION

Introduction

The expectations model offered in Chapter 2 rests on the premise that option value is formed according to investor anticipations of stock price represented as focus values. This theory attempts to relate changes in focus outcomes to the market activity of options. As such, focus values anticipated by profit-oriented investors provide a rationale for option valuation. Based on this theory, the fundamental dynamic equation was formulated for the value of an option:

$$(5.1) \qquad y(t) = \sum_{s=-b_1}^{b_2} \beta_s x_f(t-s) + \varepsilon(t),$$

where $y(t)$ is the option value for period t; $x_f(t)$ represents one of the focus values at period t; β_s is an unknown lag function with $s = -b_1, \ldots, b_2$; and $\epsilon(t)$ is white noise.

The goal of the present chapter is to determine the lag function β_s in (5.1) that best fits the warrant price data described in Chapter 4. Testing the fundamental equation, however, is only possible if (1) a specific form of the lag function is known a priori and (2) all values of s are non-negative so that efficient estimation algorithms may be applied.

This latter problem can be resolved by examining the cross correlation function $r_k[\varepsilon(t{:}x_f); \varepsilon(t{:}y)]$ computed by the two-stage scheme. If estimates are nonzero for negative lags of order $|-b_1|$, the convention adopted will be to shift the x_f series backward $|-b_1|$ periods, as described in the section on two-stage identification. Letting $b^* = b_2 + b_1$, equation (5.1) may be rewritten as

$$(5.2) \qquad y(t) = \sum_{s=0}^{b^*} \beta_s x_f(t-s) + \varepsilon(t).$$

Of course, if the estimates are nonzero only for positive lags of order b_2, then $b^* = b_2$.

The basic strategy of model specification to be followed relies on the notion of rational lag functions, so that equation (5.2) can be written as

$$y(t) = \frac{\alpha(B)}{\alpha(B)} x_f(t) + \varepsilon(t), \tag{5.3}$$

where $\alpha(B)$, $\beta(B)$ represent two finite polynomials of unknown order a and b respectively (a and b being non-negative integers):

$$\alpha(B) = 1 - \alpha_1 B - \cdots - \alpha_a B^a \tag{5.4a}$$

and

$$\beta(B) = \beta_0 + \beta_1 B + \cdots + \beta_b B^b. \tag{5.4b}$$

The purpose of this step is to introduce a class of lag functions to represent a wide range of dependence. Because each hypothesis a, b implies something different about the influence of expectations, one can obtain several alternative and competing testable forms of the fundamental equation. Given this class of expectations hypotheses, statistical analysis permits the selection of a particular model form as being most relevant for a set of data. Once a model of order a, b has been identified, the coefficients α_s, β_s can be efficiently estimated. It should be possible to approximate any arbitrary lag function to any desired degree of accuracy by a member of this a, b class. In addition, the number of parameters required for a satisfactory approximation will be small. This is important because of the relatively small number of observations available for warrants and also because of the possibility of mutually correlated lag variables.

This chapter begins with an example of the general methodology employed. Attention is then directed to identifying an expectations relationship by inspecting estimated cross correlation functions for the entire sample of warrants. Next, emphasis is placed on determining efficient parameter estimates because the correlations tend to follow a recognizable pattern over time. Finally, the empirical results are tabulated and discussed.

An Example of the Methodology

Consider the warrant of Avco Corporation. We want to examine how the focus high series $x_h(t)$ for Avco might be related to the warrant series $y_c(t)$. The available data consist of monthly values from March 1969 to September 1973 for both the warrant and the focus high series.

Relating the Two Series

The two-stage procedure of model identification discussed earlier will now be illustrated. Each of the univariate series $y_c(t)$, $x_h(t)$ was previously fitted in using the ARMA(p, q) class of models. Hence, the transformations

$$\text{(5.5a)} \qquad \begin{aligned} \varepsilon(t:y_c) &= y_c(t) \\ \hat{\sigma}^2\varepsilon(t:y_c) &= .2178\text{E–01} \qquad (54\text{df}) \end{aligned}$$

$$\text{(5.5b)} \qquad \begin{aligned} \varepsilon(t:x_h) &= \frac{x_h(t)}{\underset{(.137)}{(1 + .246B} - \underset{(.139)}{.219B^2)}} \\ \hat{\sigma}^2\varepsilon(t:x_h) &= .1197\text{E–01} \qquad (54\text{df}) \end{aligned}$$

were applied to the series $y_c(t)$ and $x_h(t)$ to yield the white noise series $\varepsilon(t:y_c)$ and $\varepsilon(t:x_h)$.

At the second stage of identification the two white noise series $\varepsilon(t:x_h)$ and $\varepsilon(t:y_c)$ are cross correlated. The estimated cross correlations are plotted in Figure 8. One and two standard error limits, given the hypothesis that the series are independent, are also shown.

There is some evidence of significant positive correlation at lags $k = 0, -1$; and a model of the form

$$\text{(5.6)} \qquad \varepsilon(t:y_c) = (\beta_0 - \beta_1 B)\varepsilon(t + 1:x_h) + \varepsilon(t)$$

could possibly provide an adequate representation of the data where $\varepsilon(t)$ is an error term which in general would not be white noise.

Fitting the Model

Most of the efficient estimation routines are invalid for dynamic models containing negative lags. Therefore, as explained in the section dealing with two-stage identification in Chapter 3, the convention adopted is to shift the focus high series backward one period. The new cross correlation estimates are shown in Figure 9. It should be noted that the basic dependence structure has not been altered. Now, using the response function discussed in the section on parameter estimation, initial estimates for $\hat{\beta}_0, \hat{\beta}_1$ can be obtained by substituting values of the weights

$$\text{(5.7)} \qquad \begin{aligned} \hat{g}_k &= \frac{\sqrt{.2178\text{E–01}}}{\sqrt{.1197\text{E–01}}}\, r_k[\varepsilon(t:x_h);\, \varepsilon(t:y_c)] \\ &= 1.34\, r_k[\varepsilon(t:x_h);\, \varepsilon(t:y_c)] \end{aligned}$$

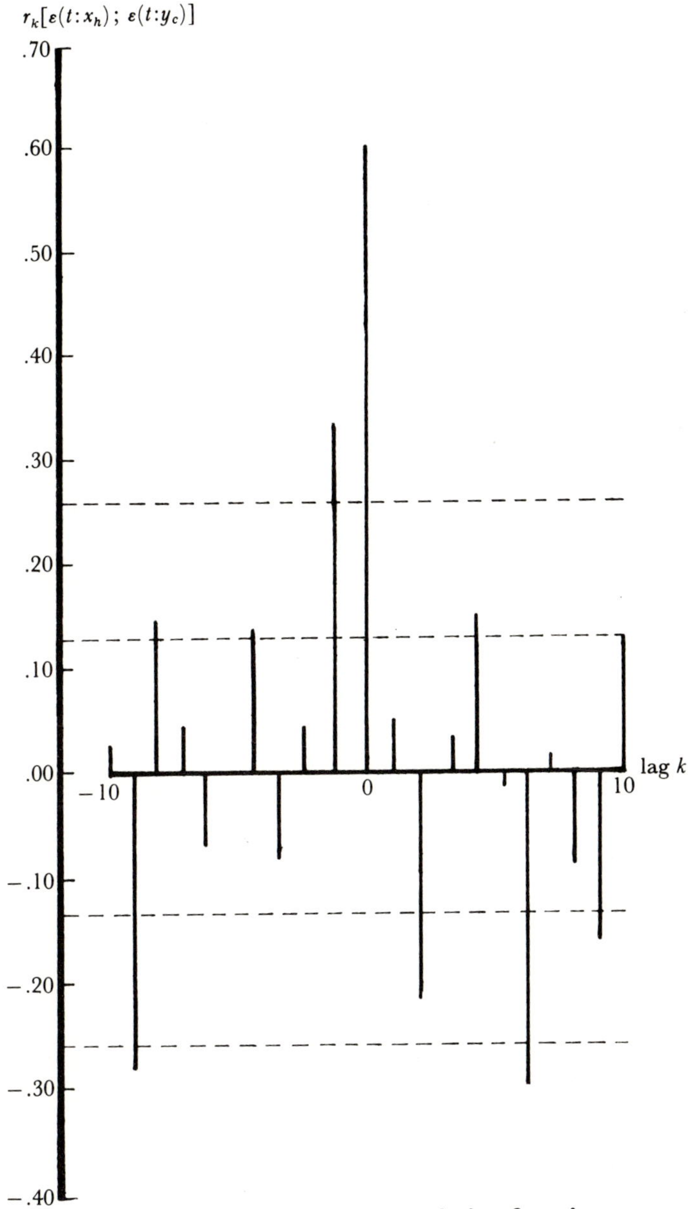

Fig. 8 Estimated cross correlation function $r_k[\varepsilon(t:x_h);\ \varepsilon(t:y_c)]$ for Avco Corporation
($N^{-1/2} = 0.13$)

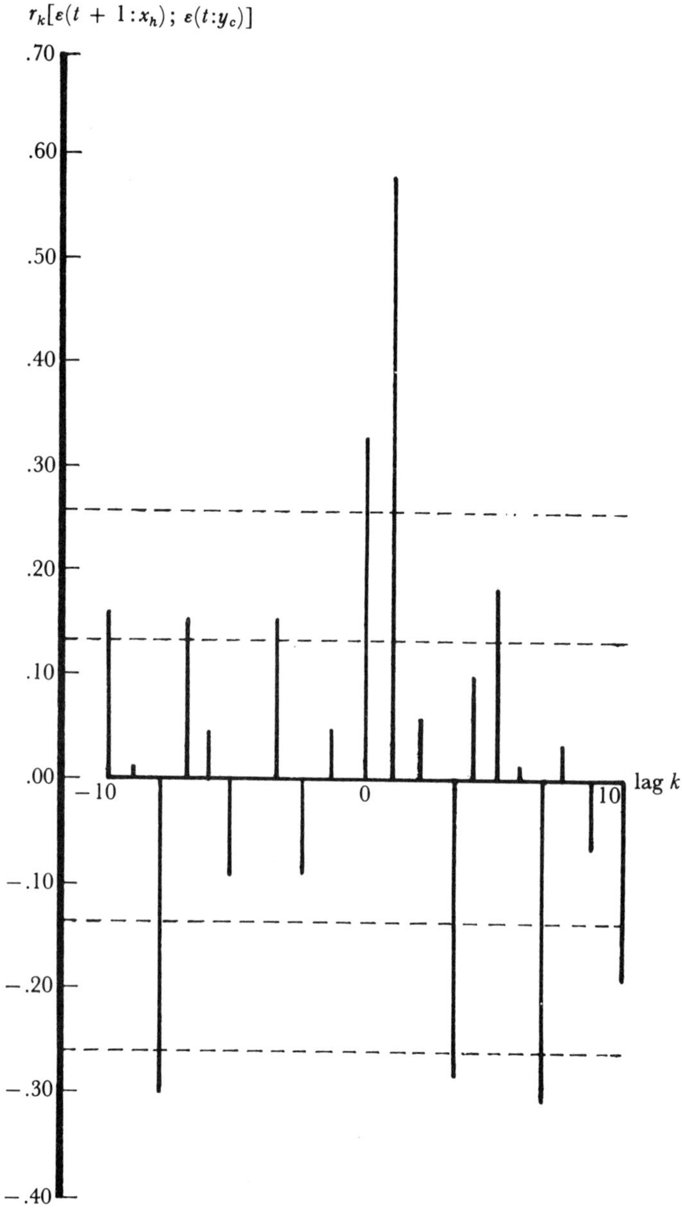

Fig. 9 Estimated cross correlation function
$r_k[\varepsilon(t+1:x_h);\ \varepsilon(t:y_c)]$ **for Avco Corporation**
($N^{-1/2} = 0.13$)

into (3.28) and solving in terms of the parameters. These estimates give the preliminary model form

$$\varepsilon(t{:}y_c) = (.469 + .764B)\varepsilon(t + 1{:}x_h) + \varepsilon(t). \tag{5.8}$$

To complete identification of the model, the two univariate series $\varepsilon(t{:}y_c)$ and $\varepsilon(t{:}x_h)$ are substituted into (5.8), yielding

$$y_c(t) = \frac{(.469 + .764B)}{(1 + .246B - .219B^2)}\, x_h(t + 1) + \varepsilon(t). \tag{5.9}$$

The model form (5.9) can now be efficiently estimated by nonlinear least squares, and a fitted model[1] obtained:

$$y_c(t) = \frac{\overset{(.136)\quad(.218)}{(.422 + .678B)}}{\underset{(.255)\quad(.187)}{(1 - .027B + .091B^2)}}\, x_h(t + 1) + \varepsilon(t) \tag{5.10}$$

$$\hat{\sigma}^2\varepsilon(t) = .1103\text{E–}01 \qquad (49\text{df}).$$

Note that, as for other estimation results given later, some initial observations were dropped from the series to facilitate calculation of model residuals in the iterative nonlinear least squares routine that was used. The parameter estimates are approximate or conditional least square estimates, and the standard errors reported in parentheses are obtained by assuming model linearity in the region of parameter convergence. The degrees of freedom (df) are calculated as the difference between the number of residuals appearing in the sum of squares to be minimized and the number of parameters estimated. Initial parameter estimates used in the iterative estimation method are those obtained previously.

In sum, the estimates $\hat{\alpha}_1$ and $\hat{\alpha}_2$ are small compared with their standard errors, but $\hat{\beta}_0$ and $\hat{\beta}_1$ are large relative to their standard errors, indicating that there is real dependence between the two series.

Further Modeling

The above fitting procedure was carried out under the assumption of uncorrelated disturbances. In order to determine whether this assumption is appropriate, the residuals $\varepsilon(t)$ should be examined. The estimated

1. For results reported in this chapter and Chapter 6, the shifting procedure employed (see the section on two-stage identification in Chapter 3) may alter the various sampling distributions on which inferences are based.

autocorrelation function of the residuals $r_k[\varepsilon(t)]$ is shown in Table 5(a). The autocorrelations exhibit a pattern suggestive of the process

$$\varepsilon(t) = \frac{n(t)}{(1 + .382B)}. \tag{5.11}$$

An examination of the residual cross correlations $r_k[\varepsilon(t + 1:x_h), n(t)]$ between the transformed focus high series and the residuals indicates possible correlation at lag $k = 6$.

Taking these adjustments into account, a further application of the nonlinear fitting procedure yielded the model

$$\text{(5.12a)} \quad \begin{aligned} y_c(t) &= \underset{(0.99)}{(4.92} + \underset{(.098)}{.688B} - \underset{(.092)}{.264B^7)}x_h(t + 1) + \frac{n(t)}{\underset{(.132)}{(1 + .455B)}} \\ \hat{\sigma}^2 n(t) &= .7883\text{E–}02 \qquad (49\text{df}). \end{aligned}$$

Equation (5.12a) may also be written in the format

$$\text{(5.12b)} \quad \begin{aligned} y_c(t) = {} & -.455y_c(t - 1) + .492x_h(t + 1) + .912x_h(t) \\ & + .313x_h(t - 1) - .264x_h(t - 6) - .120x_h(t - 7) + n(t). \end{aligned}$$

Checking the Model

In order to determine whether the dependence between the two series $y_c(t)$ and $x_h(t + 1)$ has been adequately represented by (5.12), autocorrelation and cross correlation checks should again be applied. Table 5(b) shows the sample autocorrelations $r_k[n(t)]$ of the residuals. The sample cross correlations $r_k[\varepsilon(t + 1:x_h); n(t)]$ are shown in Table 5(c). Using the results of Pierce (1968), rough overall tests can be obtained. Comparison of the values

$$Q = \sum_{k=1}^{30} r_k^2[n(t)] = 13.6, \tag{5.13a}$$

$$S(+\text{lag}) = \sum_{k=0}^{30} r_k[\varepsilon(t + 1:x_h); n(t)] = 21.8, \tag{5.13b}$$

and

$$S(-\text{lag}) = \sum_{k=-30}^{-1} r_k[\varepsilon(t + 1:x_h); n(t)] = 18.0, \tag{5.13c}$$

with tabulated values of χ^2 having 29, 27, 31 degrees of freedom, and with Table 5, provides little evidence of the need to employ a model more

TABLE 5

DIAGNOSTIC CHECKS FOR AVCO EXAMPLE OF FUNDAMENTAL DYNAMIC MODEL

lag k	0	1	2	3	4	5	6	7	8	9	10	Q
					(a) ESTIMATED AUTOCORRELATION FUNCTION $r_k[\varepsilon(t)]$							
0 to 10	1.00	−.38	.05	.13	−.21	.12	.06	−.11	.00	.16	−.17	15.45
11 to 20		.16	−.05	.05	−.11	−.01	.06	−.07	.17	−.16	−.02	21.29
21 to 30		−.05	−.02	−.07	−.08	.12	−.09	−.06	.00	.04	−.03	23.50
					(b) ESTIMATED AUTOCORRELATION FUNCTION $r_k[n(t)]$							
0 to 10	1.00	−.06	−.05	.14	−.21	.01	.06	−.12	.14	.23	−.08	8.90
11 to 20		.11	−.06	−.03	−.03	−.07	−.04	−.01	.11	−.09	−.03	11.37
21 to 30		−.08	−.07	−.09	−.09	.06	−.07	.01	.01	.07	−.04	13.57

lag k	0	1	2	3	4	5	6	7	8	9	10	S
					(c) ESTIMATED CROSS CORRELATION FUNCTION $r_k[\varepsilon(t+1:x_h);\, n(t)]$							
0 to 10	.01	−.02	.03	.01	.13	.20	.01	−.10	.17	−.03	−.17	7.07
11 to 20		.02	−.18	−.15	.01	.06	.12	−.04	−.01	−.05	−.13	12.16
21 to 30		.00	.14	−.09	−.19	−.24	.04	.21	.00	−.06	.10	21.79
−1 to −10		.13	.03	.18	.04	−.04	.19	.20	−.21	.00	.12	11.75
−11 to −20		.03	.03	−.03	−.10	.11	.16	−.07	−.12	−.07	−.09	16.02
−21 to −30		−.01	−.09	−.04	.04	−.04	−.01	−.09	.09	.04	−.08	18.03

elaborate than (5.12). Figure 10 graphs the fitted model (after converting the price changes back to normalized prices) against the actual normalized warrant series.

In summary, it appears that the dynamic modeling procedure has indicated an adequate model form for the data. Recall that $\hat{\sigma}^2\varepsilon(t{:}y_c) =$ .2178E–01, so the dynamic expectations model (5.12) has reduced the noise variance by approximately 64 percent to .7883E–02. Thus, the focus high series does seem to be of some value in explaining the stochastic behavior of the warrant series.

Relationships Between Price and Focus Value

Now we will look at the remaining warrants. Two-stage identification provides a means of examining the expectations hypotheses. It accomplishes this task by specifying the price–focus value relationship over time, as well as determining causality between price and focus values. Following this procedure, cross correlation estimates were computed between each of the white noise series $\varepsilon(t{:}x_c)$, $\varepsilon(t{:}x_h)$, and $\varepsilon(t{:}x_l)$ and the white noise series $\varepsilon(t{:}y_c)$. It is assumed that the original series $x_c(t)$, $x_h(t)$, $x_l(t)$, and $y_c(t)$ have each been transformed to white noise by an appropriate ARMA(p, q) model. Table 6 and Appendix C feature the estimated cross correlations for the warrant population.

It was assumed in discussion of the fundamental dynamic equation (Chapter 2) that an option is nearly perfectly correlated with its associated stock. The estimates of $r_k[\varepsilon(t{:}x_c)\,;\,\varepsilon(t{:}y_c)]$, which are nearly one at lag $k =$ 0, confirm this hypothesis. There is no evidence of further dependence between the common and the warrant at other lags.

A systematic examination of the estimates $r_k[\varepsilon(t{:}x_h)\,;\,\varepsilon(t{:}y_c)]$ and $r_k[\varepsilon(t{:}x_l)\,;\,\varepsilon(t{:}y_c)]$ reveals the occurrence of significant lags for $k = 0, -1$. The majority of these correlations is large compared with their respective standard errors, $N^{-1/2}$ under the assumption of series independence. There is evidence that the correlations $r_k[\varepsilon(t{:}x_h)\,;\,\varepsilon(t{:}y_c)]$ at lag $k = -1$ are about half the size of the estimates at lag $k = 0$. For the correlations $r_k[\varepsilon(t{:}x_l)\,;\,\varepsilon(t{:}y_c)]$ the estimates at lag $k = 0$ and at lag $k = -1$ are similar in size.

Patterns of this sort suggest that models of the following form may be appropriate for either focus value x_f:

$$\varepsilon(t{:}y_c) = (\beta_0 + \beta_1 B)\varepsilon(t + 1{:}x_f) \tag{5.14}$$

and

$$(1 - \alpha_1 B)\varepsilon(t{:}y_c) = \beta_0\varepsilon(t + 1{:}x_f). \tag{5.15}$$

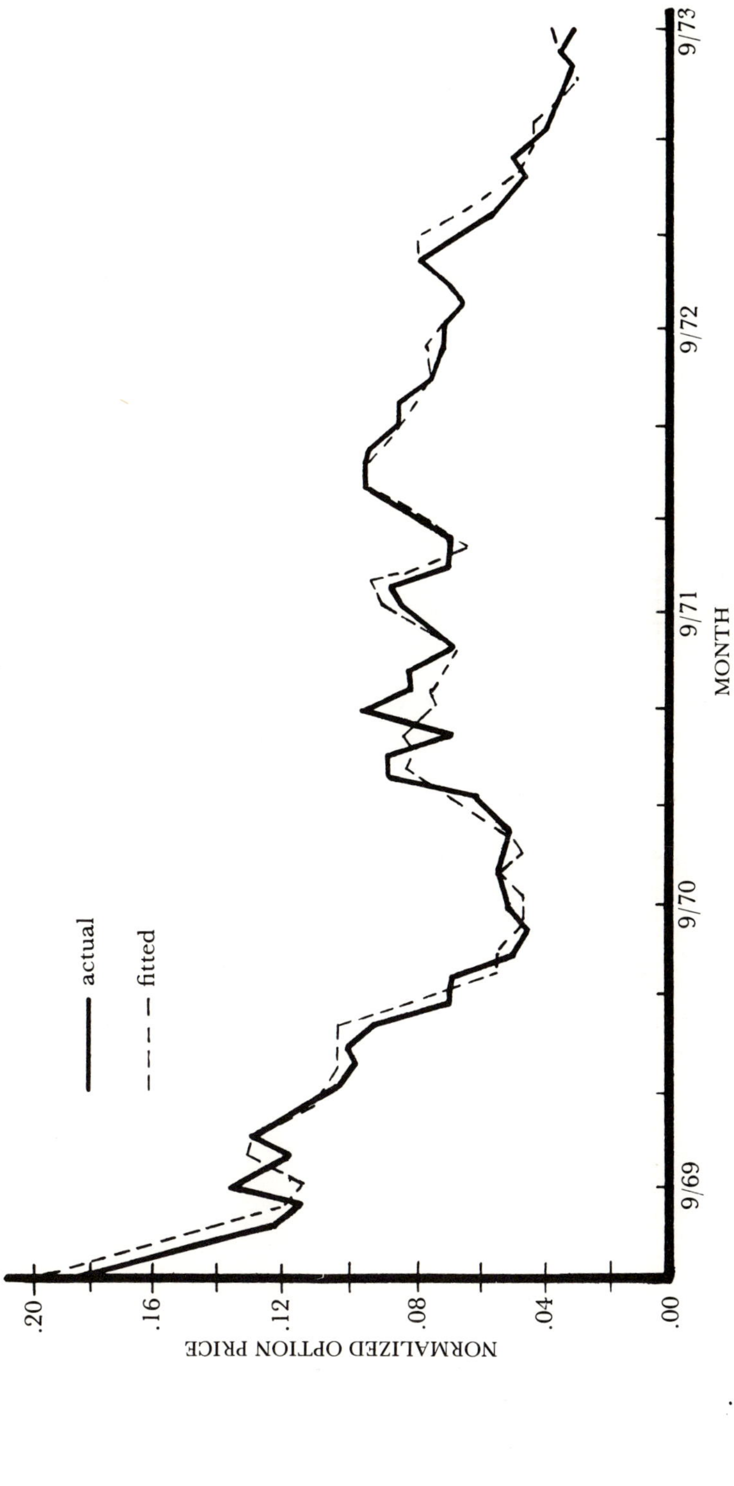

Fig. 10 Fitted fundamental dynamic model for Avco example

TABLE 6

RELATIONSHIPS BETWEEN PRICE AND FOCUS VALUE

WARRANT	LAGS	0	1	2	3	4	5	6	7	8	9	10
	(a) ESTIMATED CROSS CORRELATION FUNCTION $r_k[\varepsilon(t:x_c); \varepsilon(t:y_c)]$											
Allegheny Airlines (1987)	0 to 10	.90	.01	−.05	−.04	.02	−.06	−.31	.11	.02	.09	.05
	−1 to −10		.07	−.13	−.15	.06	−.06	−.23	.02	.08	.04	.01
American Telephone & Telegraph	0 to 10	.84	−.03	.07	.05	−.21	−.11	−.05	−.27	.00	−.01	−.14
	−1 to −10		.14	−.16	−.10	−.11	−.16	.00	−.15	−.11	.03	.01
Avco	0 to 10	.85	.06	−.09	.04	.05	.12	−.26	−.06	−.03	−.18	−.02
	−1 to −10		.04	−.08	.03	.10	−.03	−.18	.13	.07	−.21	.04
Gulf & Western	0 to 10	.84	.18	.19	−.02	.15	.02	.06	.09	−.26	−.02	−.07
	−1 to −10		.11	.16	.04	−.04	.04	.02	.13	−.27	.00	.02
Loews	0 to 10	.89	.13	.13	.06	.08	−.11	−.09	.01	−.13	.09	.11
	−1 to −10		.08	.17	−.02	.02	−.15	.02	−.03	−.15	.13	.10
Northwest	0 to 10	.88	.17	−.03	−.05	.11	.14	.06	.12	.04	−.12	−.03
	−1 to −10		−.07	−.04	.00	.11	.13	.12	.08	.00	−.12	−.02
Tenneco	0 to 10	.83	−.09	.30	.10	−.05	−.07	−.10	−.17	.07	−.15	−.09
	−1 to −10		−.04	.07	.06	.06	−.24	.00	−.12	−.12	.04	−.05
Trans World Airlines	0 to 10	.92	.08	.01	.02	.24	.11	.03	.08	.00	.18	−.10
	−1 to −10		.03	−.04	.10	.13	.09	.02	.09	.02	.10	−.03
	(b) ESTIMATED CROSS CORRELATION FUNCTION $r_k[\varepsilon(t:x_h); \varepsilon(t:y_c)]$											
Allegheny Airlines (1987)	0 to 10	.73	.01	−.15	.06	.04	−.15	−.32	.12	.07	.15	.04
	−1 to −10		.26	−.11	−.13	.03	−.06	−.14	−.06	.12	.03	−.05
American Telephone & Telegraph	0 to 10	.52	−.08	.23	−.15	.00	−.09	−.18	−.23	.04	−.15	.10
	−1 to −10		.45	−.13	−.17	−.02	−.18	.00	−.10	−.05	−.02	−.07
Avco	0 to 10	.61	.04	−.21	.05	.15	−.01	−.30	.04	−.09	−.16	.13
	−1 to −10		.33	.04	−.10	.16	−.02	−.08	.06	.15	−.29	.02

Gulf & Western	0 to 10	.64	.16	.04	.13	.09	.02	.07	−.07	−.11	.01	−.02
	−1 to −10		.34	.01	.17	−.01	−.01	−.02	.13	−.17	−.13	.16
Loews	0 to 10	.57	−.03	.23	−.02	−.00	−.14	.07	−.21	.11	.08	.07
	−1 to −10		.42	.12	−.02	−.02	−.03	.02	−.06	−.02	−.04	.16
Northwest	0 to 10	.72	−.01	.03	−.03	.10	.16	.05	.11	.01	−.07	−.08
	−1 to −10		.22	.06	−.07	.17	.09	.20	.14	−.05	−.10	.00
Tenneco	0 to 10	.49	−.01	.33	−.03	.00	−.14	−.03	−.24	.11	−.16	−.06
	−1 to −10		.24	.00	.15	−.01	−.13	.03	−.06	−.21	.03	−.03
Trans World Airlines	0 to 10	.68	−.01	.03	.14	.22	.01	.04	.13	.09	.03	−.02
	−1 to −10		.31	.09	.14	.07	.06	−.02	.11	.14	.00	.00
	(c) ESTIMATED CROSS CORRELATION FUNCTION $r_k[\varepsilon(t:x_i);\ \varepsilon(t:y_c)]$											
Allegheny Airlines (1987)	0 to 10	.36	.04	−.02	−.07	.02	−.21	−.11	.00	.17	.03	.13
	−1 to −10		.61	−.17	−.09	−.08	−.02	−.12	−.14	.14	.03	.05
American Telephone & Telegraph	0 to 10	.44	−.11	.13	−.08	−.12	−.09	−.09	−.31	.06	−.01	.09
	−1 to −10		.60	.00	−.11	−.05	−.19	−.14	.15	−.18	−.16	.13
Avco	0 to 10	.46	.11	−.11	.07	.14	−.15	−.20	.06	−.11	−.30	.15
	−1 to −10		.56	−.11	.06	.05	.06	−.12	.05	.08	−.18	.01
Gulf & Western	0 to 10	.48	.18	.05	.21	.00	.02	.08	.06	−.21	.01	−.02
	−1 to −10		.50	−.06	.14	.01	−.02	−.02	.06	−.05	−.15	.05
Loews	0 to 10	.48	.23	.05	.19	−.10	.05	−.11	.05	−.17	.11	.10
	−1 to −10		.42	−.16	.08	.06	−.10	.03	−.05	.00	−.06	.30
Northwest	0 to 10	.52	.14	−.14	.08	.13	.05	.13	.12	−.06	−.06	−.01
	−1 to −10		.43	−.02	−.12	.20	−.03	.14	.24	.02	−.10	−.09
Tenneco	0 to 10	.53	.05	.19	.02	−.13	−.11	−.08	−.05	−.10	−.08	.08
	−1 to −10		.38	−.08	.26	−.01	−.10	−.12	−.01	−.15	−.09	.04
Trans World Airlines	0 to 10	.55	.05	.03	.10	.13	.13	.03	.01	.09	.04	−.03
	−1 to −10		.50	−.16	.01	.16	.11	.03	.03	.09	.05	.06

Graphic illustrations of the response functions for these specific models are shown in Figure 11. The first model would imply that the response function is spread over two months in proportion to the values β_0 and β_1. In the second model, the response function tails off exponentially from the initial starting value β_0.

Although these initial observations suggest a definite pattern between focus value changes and changes in the warrant price, further discussion of these relations will be deferred until efficient estimates of the parameters have been obtained.[2]

Fundamental Dynamic Equations

The present section summarizes the results of efficiently fitting the identified model forms by iterative least squares procedures. It is assumed that starting values for the nonlinear estimation routine have been obtained as described in the section in Chapter 3 on parameter estimation.

The results of the estimation phase are reported for each of the eight warrants listed in Table 2. Separate models have been fitted for the focus high and the focus low. The accompanying Tables 7 and 11 list (1) the warrant considered, (2) the estimated models, and (3) criteria for judging the quality of the explanation, including standard errors for the estimates, the residual variance, degrees of freedom, and the Durbin–Watson statistic. Additional tables are provided which list the residual autocorrelations of each model and compute the statistics Q, $S(+\text{lag})$, $S(-\text{lag})$ suggested by Pierce (1968) to determine the goodness of fit (see Tables 8, 9, 12, and 13).

Note that, in the criteria included in the tables, the residual variance that evaluates the overall significance of the fitted models has been adjusted for loss of degrees of freedom. To illustrate why this was done, consider the variance of the disturbances. The estimation criterion of minimum sum of squares (i.e., equation 3.23) may equivalently be thought of as the criterion of minimum variance of residuals. Now generally the addition of a parameter to a model may be expected to reduce the sum of squares in (3.23), and hence the residual variance, because the additional parameter offers one additional degree of freedom along which to reduce them. Consequently, to penalize the model for its use of parameters or degrees of freedom, one may compute estimates of the residual variance by dividing the sum of squares by the number of observations less the number of parameters to obtain the net remaining degrees of freedom.

The significance of the estimated parameters can be tested by forming

2. See Box and Jenkins (1970) for additional illustrations of response functions that are likely to occur in practice.

First Model: $\varepsilon(t{:}y_c) = (\beta_0 + \beta_1 B)\varepsilon(t + 1{:}x_f)$

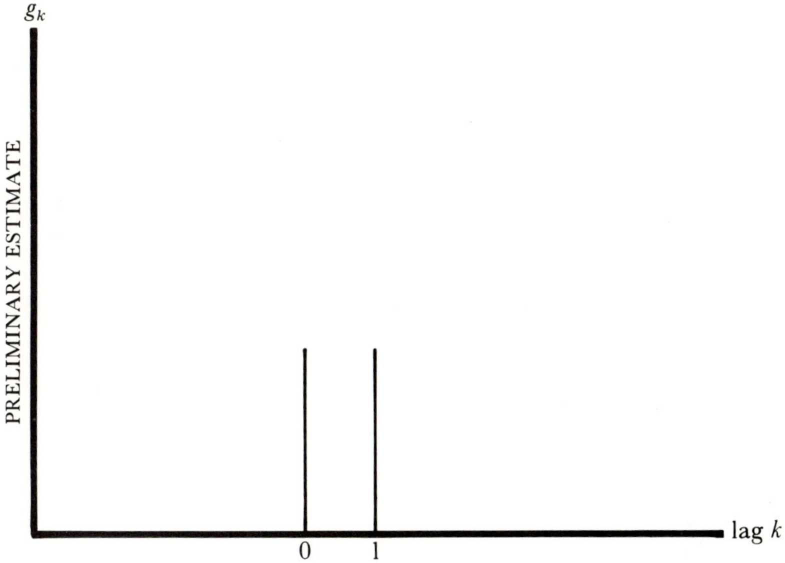

Second Model: $(1 - \alpha_1 B)\varepsilon(t{:}y_c) = \beta_0\varepsilon(t + 1{:}x_f)$

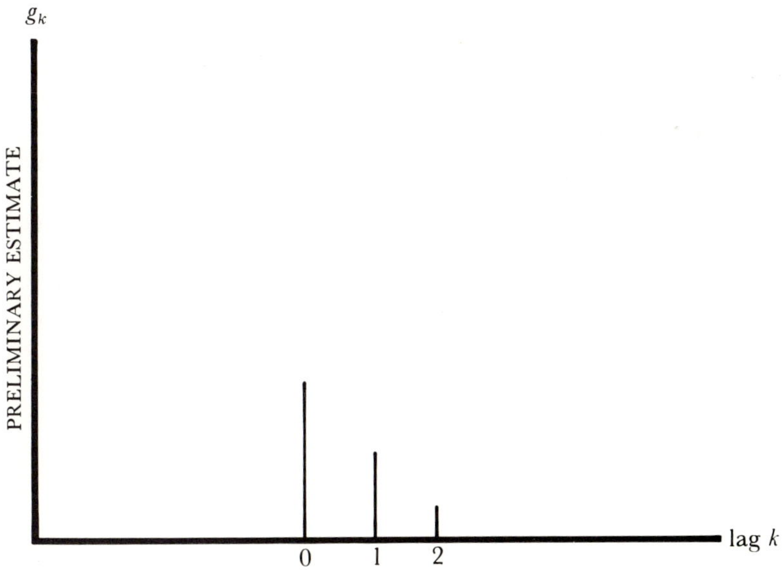

Fig. 11 Illustrative response functions

the ratio of the estimated parameters to their standard errors, termed the z ratio. This ratio enables us to test the null hypothesis that the true value of the estimated parameters is zero. One can also assign confidence limits for the parameter estimates by referring to this ratio. The z ratio is approximately normally distributed on the assumption of a white noise error term. The probability that a standard normal variable lies outside the bounds ± 1.96 is .05. To test the hypothesis that an estimated coefficient is significant, one can simply compare the z ratio to the value 1.96 or approximately 2.00.

Several difficulties arise in interpreting the results presented. With regard to the models, the major difficulty is the feedback situation observed in the previous section. As a result, each of the focus value series was shifted backward one period. Then the cross correlation functions were re-estimated to obtain the starting values for the iterative routine. This shifting procedure may alter the various sampling distributions on which inferences are based.

Another problem is that the lagged values of the focus values may be highly intercorrelated. Multicollinearity can produce imprecise estimates of the lagged coefficients and their variances, thus making significance measures imprecise. Fitted models which had parameter estimates that were highly correlated are not reported.

A third difficulty involves the testing of the autocorrelative properties of the regression residuals. Autocorrelation in the residuals implies that fitted price changes are systematically above or below actual price change. The quantity Q devised by Pierce (1968) is especially useful for testing autocorrelation where the Durbin–Watson statistic is only marginally applicable—for instance, in models containing lagged dependent variables. The Q statistic offers a test of the smallness of a whole set of sample autocorrelations.

Finally, each of the identified models was first fitted to the data under the assumption of a white noise error term. The resulting residuals were examined for autocorrelation. When appropriate, an ARMA(p, q) model was incorporated for the error term, and estimation was repeated.

Results for Focus High

Table 7 lists the models fitted by efficient estimation techniques to warrant prices in relation to focus highs. The residual autocorrelations for each model are given in Table 8.

The data appear to support the basic form (5.14). The coefficients β_0 and β_1 were positive for all warrants. Standard errors for each of the coefficients represent a degree of assurance that the true value of the parameters lies in the region specified. Both the residual autocorrelations

Table 7
FUNDAMENTAL DYNAMIC MODELS FOR FOCUS HIGH

Warrant/(a, b_1, b_2)	Fitted Models	Residual Variance	df	DW
Allegheny Airlines (1987) (0, 1, 1)	$y_c(t) = (\underset{(.102)}{.293} + \underset{(.128)}{1.047}B - \underset{(.098)}{.269}B^2)x_h(t+1) + (1 - \underset{(.105)}{.641}B)n(t)$	.1022E–01	69	1.865
American Telephone & Telegraph (0, 1, 0)	$y_c(t) = (\underset{(.307)}{1.124} + \underset{(.306)}{1.194}B)x_h(t+1) + n(t)$	.6779E–02	35	2.301
Avco (0, 1, 1)	$y_c(t) = (\underset{(.099)}{.492} + \underset{(.098)}{.688}B - \underset{(.092)}{.264}B^7)x_h(t+1) + \dfrac{n(t)}{(1 + \underset{(.132)}{.455}B)}$	.7883E–02	49	2.059
Gulf & Western (0, 1, 0)	$y_c(t) = (\underset{(.125)}{.466} + \underset{(.123)}{.894}B)x_h(t+1) + \dfrac{n(t)}{(1 + \underset{(.108)}{.483}B)}$	.1016E–01	63	1.775
Loews (0, 1, 0)	$y_c(t) = (\underset{(.128)}{.771} + \underset{(.129)}{.681}B)x_h(t+1) + \dfrac{n(t)}{(1 + \underset{(.127)}{.714}B + \underset{(.138)}{.403}B^2)}$	.9068E–02	52	2.088
Loews (1, 1, 0)	$y_c(t) = \dfrac{(\overset{(.129)}{.703} + \overset{(.175)}{1.244}B)}{(1 + \underset{(.135)}{.414}B)}x_h(t+1) + \dfrac{n(t)}{(1 + \underset{(.125)}{.684}B + \underset{(.130)}{.459}B^2)}$	.8539E–02	51	2.126

(continued)

Note: (a, b_1, b_2) indicates a order lagged dependent variables, b_1 order leading independent variables, and b_2 order lagged independent variables. Standard errors are shown by parameter estimates. Residual variances are expressed in real exponential form. Degrees of freedom are denoted by df, and DW denotes the Durbin and Watson statistic.

TABLE 7 *Continued*

WARRANT/(a, b_1, b_2)	FITTED MODELS	RESIDUAL VARIANCE	df	DW
Northwest (0, 1, 0)	$y_c(t) = \underset{(.172)}{(.501} + \underset{(.165)}{1.089B)}x_h(t+1) + (1 - \underset{(.134)}{.567B})n(t)$	.8721E–02	42	1.913
Tenneco (0, 1, 1)	$y_c(t) = \underset{(.174)}{(.366} + \underset{(.181)}{.740B} + \underset{(.166)}{.364B^3)}x_h(t+1) + (1 - \underset{(.136)}{.389B})n(t)$	.6030E–02	48	1.917
Tenneco (2, 1, 0)	$y_c(t) = \dfrac{\overset{(.159)}{(.418} + \overset{(.165)}{.878B)}}{(1 + \underset{(.121)}{.311B} - \underset{(.119)}{.440B^2})}\, x_h(t+1) + (1 - \underset{(.141)}{.355B})n(t)$	.6079E–02	46	1.885
Trans World Airlines (0, 1, 2)	$y_c(t) = \underset{(.073)}{(.490} + \underset{(.079)}{.998B} - \underset{(.072)}{.239B^3} + \underset{(.064)}{.233B^5)}x_h(t+1) + (1 - \underset{(.069)}{.624B})n(t)$	.1133E–01	134	2.156

TABLE 8
RESIDUAL AUTOCORRELATIONS FOR FOCUS HIGH MODELS FITTED IN TABLE 7

WARRANT/(a, b_1, b_2)	LAGS	1	2	3	4	5	6	7	8	9	10
Allegheny Airlines (1987)	1 to 10	.05	.01	−.07	−.08	.00	−.08	.08	.13	.00	−.04
(0, 1, 1)	11 to 20	.03	−.07	−.05	.10	.72	.07	−.04	−.06	−.08	.00
American Telephone &	1 to 10	−.18	.09	.09	−.10	−.15	.26	−.04	.05	.31	−.16
Telegraph (0, 1, 0)	11 to 20	.19	.04	−.06	−.05	.19	−.21	.04	.07	−.08	−.01
Avco (0, 1, 1)	1 to 10	−.06	−.05	.14	−.21	.01	.06	−.13	.14	.23	−.08
	11 to 20	.11	−.06	−.03	−.03	−.07	−.04	−.01	.11	−.09	−.03
Gulf & Western (0, 1, 0)	1 to 10	.08	−.04	−.09	−.09	−.06	.09	.19	−.13	−.12	−.20
	11 to 20	−.01	.06	.12	−.04	−.03	−.01	−.11	.16	.05	−.09
Loews (0, 1, 0)	1 to 10	−.06	−.07	−.15	.24	−.05	−.03	−.04	−.08	−.06	−.17
	11 to 20	.02	−.20	.12	−.09	.05	−.09	.22	−.08	.04	.11
Loews (1, 1, 0)	1 to 10	−.03	−.04	−.15	.14	.02	−.08	.03	−.14	.00	−.29
	11 to 20	.04	−.22	.11	−.05	−.02	.04	.17	.06	−.03	.10
Northwest (0, 1, 0)	1 to 10	.04	−.07	.05	−.05	−.02	−.10	.03	.08	−.08	−.04
	11 to 20	−.08	−.14	.16	.19	.15	−.09	−.15	.06	.00	−.13
Tenneco (0, 1, 0)	1 to 10	.01	.00	−.05	−.01	−.17	−.23	.24	.12	.12	.10
	11 to 20	.18	−.04	−.10	.07	−.03	−.03	.12	.19	.04	−.05
Tenneco (2, 1, 0)	1 to 10	.02	−.05	−.02	−.03	−.17	−.21	.24	.15	.11	.09
	11 to 20	.14	−.03	−.11	.06	.01	−.08	.18	.10	.10	−.06
Trans World Airlines	1 to 10	−.08	.04	.08	.00	.18	.11	−.02	−.17	.11	.01
(0, 1, 2)	11 to 20	.18	.08	−.12	.03	.19	−.02	.09	−.04	−.26	.13

TABLE 9
DIAGNOSTIC CHECKS FOR FOCUS HIGH MODELS FITTED IN TABLE 7

WARRANT/(a, b_1, b_2)	Q	df	$S(+\text{lag})$	df	$S(-\text{lag})$	df
Allegheny Airlines (1987) (0, 1, 1)	16.2	29	26.5	28	31.3	31
American Telephone & Telegraph (0, 1, 0)	15.7	30	16.5	29	11.9	31
Avco (0, 1, 1)	13.6	29	21.8	28	18.0	31
Gulf & Western (0, 1, 0)	20.5	29	17.1	29	24.6	31
Loews (0, 1, 0)	21.7	28	17.2	29	13.2	31
Loews (1, 1, 0)	18.9	28	19.0	28	15.5	31
Northwest (0, 1, 0)	11.8	29	20.4	29	15.5	31
Tenneco (0, 1, 0)	19.0	29	19.0	28	12.5	31
Tenneco (2, 1, 0)	17.9	29	15.5	27	12.9	31
Trans World Airlines (0, 1, 2)	49.2	29	22.2	27	14.4	31

and the Durbin–Watson statistics denote a lack of autocorrelation in the residuals.

Diagnostic Checking

Before accepting the above models as adequate representations of the data, autocorrelation and cross correlation checks are applied. The first 30 lags of the quantities Q, $S(+\text{lag})$ and $S(-\text{lag})$ are tabulated in Table 9. Inspection of Table 9 shows that only one suspiciously large value occurs. The value $Q = 49.2$ obtained from the fitted model for Trans World Airlines suggests some model inadequacy because the 5 percent point for χ^2 with 29 degrees of freedom is 42.6. The possible nature of this inadequacy is discussed below.

Cause of Model Inadequacy

Recall from Table 2 that Trans World Airlines is the only warrant close to maturity. Chen (1970), Chopra (1974), and others conclude that a warrant's value is not significantly affected by maturity until about three years before expiration. Evidence exists which might explain in these terms the possible inadequacy of the fitted model for Trans World Airlines.

Table 10 shows the results obtained by fitting the same model form as reported in Table 7 for three different time periods: from January 1962 until one year before maturity, until two years before maturity, and until

TABLE 10
COMPARISON OF TWA (0, 1, 2) MODELS FITTED FOR THREE DIFFERENT TIME PERIODS BEFORE MATURITY

TRANS WORLD AIRLINES	N	$\hat{\beta}_0$	$\hat{\beta}_1$	$\hat{\beta}_3$	$\hat{\beta}_5$	Q	RESIDUAL VARIANCE	df	DW
The Entire Series	139	.490	−.998	.239	−.233	49.2	.1133E–01	134	2.156
One Year Before Maturity	130	.444	−1.001	.231	−.231	49.2	.1043E–01	125	2.174
Two Years Before Maturity	118	.446	−.997	.236	−.227	42.1	.1119E–01	113	2.157
Three Years Before Maturity	106	.536	−.830	.097	−.157	19.9	.9522E–02	101	2.163

Note: The Trans World Airlines warrant expires December 1, 1973. Residual variances are expressed in real exponential form. Degrees of freedom are denoted by df, and DW denotes the Durbin and Watson statistic.

TABLE 11
FUNDAMENTAL DYNAMIC MODELS FOR FOCUS LOW

WARRANT/(a, b_1, b_2)	FITTED MODELS	RESIDUAL VARIANCE	df	DW
Allegheny Airlines (1987) (0, 1, 0)	$y_c(t) = (\underset{(.091)}{.771} + \underset{(.091)}{.681}B)x_l(t+1) + \dfrac{n(t)}{(1 + \underset{(.115)}{.604}B + \underset{(.121)}{.619}B^2 + \underset{(.120)}{.436}B^3)}$	.1127E–01	68	2.026
Allegheny Airlines (1987) (1, 0, 0)	$y_c(t) = \dfrac{\overset{(.064)}{.757}}{(1 - \underset{(.059)}{.373}B)} x_l(t+1) + \dfrac{n(t)}{(1 - \underset{(.112)}{.585}B + \underset{(.117)}{.644}B^2 + \underset{(.120)}{.446}B^3)}$	.1101E–01	68	2.008
American Telephone & Telegraph (0, 1, 0)	$y_c(t) = (\underset{(.356)}{1.709} + \underset{(.356)}{1.079}B)x_l(t+1) + n(t)$	.5992E–02	35	2.507
American Telephone & Telegraph (1, 0, 0)	$y_c(t) = \dfrac{\overset{(.331)}{1.846}}{(1 - \underset{(.135)}{.346}B)} x_l(t+1) + \dfrac{n(t)}{(1 + \underset{(.168)}{.282}B)}$	.6087E–02	34	1.925
Avco (0, 1, 2)	$y_c(t) = (\underset{(.100)}{.603} + \underset{(.099)}{.592}B + \underset{(.088)}{.215}B^5 - \underset{(.089)}{.285}B^7)x_l(t+1) + \dfrac{n(t)}{(1 + \underset{(.142)}{.434}B)}$	.7088E–02	48	2.074
Avco (1, 1, 1)	$y_c(t) = \dfrac{(\overset{(.086)}{.718} - \overset{(.056)}{.118}B^5)}{(1 - \underset{(.073)}{.451}B)} x_l(t+1) + \dfrac{n(t)}{(1 + \underset{(.134)}{.484}B + \underset{(.133)}{.431}B^2)}$	.7897E–02	48	2.131

Gulf & Western (0, 1, 0)	$y_c(t) = (\underset{(.115)}{.619} + \underset{(.114)}{.607}B)x_l(t+1) + \dfrac{n(t)}{(1 + \underset{(.115)}{.419}B)}$	.1112E–01	63	1.935
Gulf & Western (1, 0, 0)	$y_c(t) = \dfrac{\overset{(.101)}{.743}}{(1 - \underset{(.083)}{.457}B)} x_l(t+1) + \dfrac{n(t)}{(1 + \underset{(.117)}{.388}B)}$	.1160E–01	63	1.981
Loews (0, 1, 0)	$y_c(t) = (\underset{(.131)}{.503} + \underset{(.126)}{.687}B)x_l(t+1) = (1 - \underset{(.122)}{.521}B)n(t)$	.1151E–01	53	1.995
Loews (1, 0, 0)	$y_c(t) = \dfrac{\overset{(.083)}{.640}}{(1 - \underset{(.064)}{.525}B)} x_l(t+1) + (1 - \underset{(.117)}{.603}B)n(t)$	.1121E–01	53	1.846
Northwest (0, 1, 0)	$y_c(t) = (\underset{(.141)}{.525} + \underset{(.140)}{.552}B)x_l(t+1) + \dfrac{n(t)}{(1 + \underset{(.142)}{.376}B)}$	.1314E–01	42	1.913
Tenneco (0, 1, 0)	$y_c(t) = (\underset{(.181)}{.478} + \underset{(.176)}{.842}B)x_l(t+1) + (1 - \underset{(.129)}{.474}B)n(t)$	.5382E–02	48	1.987
Trans World Airlines (0, 1, 0)	$y_c(t) = (\underset{(.075)}{.655} + \underset{(.074)}{.732}B)x_l(t+1) + (1 - \underset{(.073)}{.624}B)n(t)$	.1175E–01	136	2.187

Note: (a, b_1, b_2) indicates a order lagged dependent variables, b_1 order leading independent variables, and b_2 order lagged independent variables. Standard errors are shown by parameter estimates. Residual variances are expressed in real exponential form. Degrees of freedom are denoted by df, and DW denotes the Durbin and Watson statistic.

three years before maturity. Inspection of the Q values suggests that the effect of maturity has probably accounted for the model inadequacy, all other things being equal.

Results for Focus Low

Reported in Table 11 are the fitted models between the warrant price series and the focus low series. The residual autocorrelations for each model are listed in Table 12.

As with the focus highs, the coefficients $\hat{\beta}_0$ and $\hat{\beta}_1$ are positive for each warrant. Parameter estimates are all large compared with their standard errors, thus indicating that there is real dependence between the series. For five of the warrants, the two models (5.14) and (5.15) were upheld by the data. Both models are similar for Allegheny Airlines and Loews even though a slightly better fit is possible with the form (5.15). In order to generalize a model for all warrants, the basic form (5.14) is preferable. Finally, no autocorrelation can be detected from examining the residual autocorrelations or the Durbin–Watson statistics.

Diagnostic Checks

In order to determine whether the expectations relationship has been adequately represented by the above models, the results of Pierce (1968) are again used. Comparison of the values of Q, $S(+\text{lag})$ and $S(-\text{lag})$ in Table 13 with tabulated values of χ^2 for the specified degrees of freedom provides little evidence of model inadequacy. Note that the Q statistic for Trans World Airlines is now only 18.1. A possible reason for this could be that as the warrant nears expiration, investors can be reasonably sure of the worst that can happen to them. Recall from Chapter 1 that as an option approaches maturity its value approaches the lower bound or theoretical value.

Discussion of Results and Conclusions

The major concern of this chapter has been the presentation and explanation of recently available statistical methods which are useful in specifying and estimating the expectations hypotheses based on focus values. That a relationship should exist between expected stock prices and the expected value of a warrant is generally acknowledged. How to develop a procedure to determine the influence of these expectations over time has been less clear. The methodology presented above suggests a

TABLE 12

RESIDUAL AUTOCORRELATIONS FOR FOCUS LOW MODELS FITTED IN TABLE 11

WARRANT/(a, b_1, b_2)	LAGS	1	2	3	4	5	6	7	8	9	10
Allegheny Airlines (1987)	1 to 10	−.02	−.01	−.09	−.11	.08	−.05	.16	.06	−.04	−.05
(0, 1, 0)	11 to 20	−.02	.09	.02	−.05	.06	−.08	−.04	.06	.04	.01
Allegheny Airlines (1987)	1 to 10	−.02	−.01	−.09	−.11	.08	−.03	.17	.12	−.06	−.05
(1, 0, 0)	11 to 20	−.02	.03	.03	−.03	.03	−.02	−.03	.04	.01	.02
American Telephone &	1 to 10	−.26	.17	.09	−.04	.03	−.21	−.09	.25	.08	−.13
Telegraph (0, 1, 0)	11 to 20	.30	−.08	−.02	−.08	.08	−.05	.09	−.13	.09	.05
American Telephone &	1 to 10	.03	.14	.11	.02	.09	.23	.05	.26	.09	.01
Telegraph (1, 0, 0)	11 to 20	.23	.03	−.06	−.10	.04	.04	.05	−.07	.04	.01
Avco (0, 1, 2)	1 to 10	−.06	−.17	−.14	−.15	.14	.12	.05	.03	−.01	−.16
	11 to 20	.05	−.04	.07	.05	−.07	−.11	−.05	.04	−.04	.05
Avco (1, 1, 1)	1 to 10	−.08	−.11	−.13	−.03	.14	−.04	.14	.04	−.05	−.11
	11 to 20	.08	−.12	.07	−.08	−.02	−.02	−.07	.03	−.18	.01
Gulf & Western (0, 1, 0)	1 to 10	.01	−.14	−.11	.03	.01	.01	.00	−.28	.07	−.01
	11 to 20	−.03	−.08	.00	.03	.16	.08	−.11	.05	−.05	−.01
Gulf & Western (1, 0, 0)	1 to 10	−.02	−.18	−.06	.00	.00	.07	.08	−.29	.06	.00
	11 to 20	−.02	.03	−.06	−.10	.14	.07	−.11	.03	.02	−.07
Loews (0, 1, 0)	1 to 10	.00	.05	−.10	.11	−.08	−.04	−.04	−.12	−.09	−.21
	11 to 20	.02	−.18	.11	.07	.14	−.03	.24	−.02	−.01	.05
Loews (1, 0, 0)	1 to 10	.07	−.07	−.10	.12	−.05	.01	.04	−.07	−.05	−.11
	11 to 20	.04	−.17	.04	.00	.03	−.05	.20	.00	.08	.07
Northwest (0, 1, 0)	1 to 10	.00	−.11	−.01	−.06	−.07	−.05	.07	.13	−.14	−.07
	11 to 20	.07	−.19	.10	.11	.02	−.07	−.22	−.13	−.07	−.06
Tenneco (0, 1, 0)	1 to 10	−.02	.09	−.06	−.01	−.14	−.09	−.01	.11	.17	.03
	11 to 20	.23	.04	−.05	.10	.02	.14	.08	.11	−.08	−.04
Trans World Airlines	1 to 10	−.11	.10	.11	.02	.02	−.06	.10	−.09	.05	−.10
(0, 1, 0)	11 to 20	.08	.04	.00	.04	.11	−.05	.03	.05	−.01	.05

TABLE 13
DIAGNOSTIC CHECKS FOR FOCUS LOW MODELS FITTED IN TABLE 11

WARRANT/(a, b_1, b_2)	Q	df	$S(+\text{lag})$	df	$S(-\text{lag})$	df
Allegheny Airlines (1987) (0, 1, 0)	15.2	27	13.9	29	30.9	31
Allegheny Airlines (1987) (1, 0, 0)	14.7	27	14.6	29	31.0	31
American Telephone & Telegraph (0, 1, 0)	15.5	30	10.0	29	16.4	31
American Telephone & Telegraph (1, 0, 0)	10.7	29	13.8	29	16.8	31
Avco (0, 1, 2)	12.4	29	22.3	27	29.6	31
Avco (1, 1, 1)	10.4	28	24.6	28	26.0	31
Gulf & Western (0, 1, 0)	20.3	29	24.4	29	16.0	31
Gulf & Western (1, 0, 0)	19.5	29	23.1	29	19.1	31
Loews (0, 1, 0)	16.0	29	19.3	29	15.6	31
Loews (1, 0, 0)	9.4	29	16.4	29	21.7	31
Northwest (0, 1, 0)	13.0	29	15.5	29	25.8	31
Tenneco (0, 1, 0)	14.6	29	10.1	29	18.9	31
Trans World Airlines (0, 1, 0)	18.1	29	20.9	29	30.2	31

procedure for specifying models to explain warrant behavior dynamically, including the use of expectations.[3]

From the results, the following inferences can be drawn.

1. The major conclusion of this chapter is that stock price expectations have an important influence on warrant value. Changing investor expectations of stock price were found to be positively related to warrant price changes for all eight companies. This supports the earlier work of Sprenkle (1961) and Black and Scholes (1973); however, it does not necessarily support their explanation of why the relationship exists. For instance, Sprenkle had difficulty in estimating expected stock prices, so he assumed that they were close to the current price of the stock. Our argument that actual market prices are formed by human decisions concerning focus outcomes seems more plausible. This line of reasoning

3. Each of the fundamental dynamic equations in this chapter was also fitted by applying the influence of the senior security directly to the exercise price, as indicated in the third footnote of Chapter 4. In all models the form of the response functions was identical to those reported in Tables 7 and 11, but the magnitude of the coefficients was slightly smaller. As a result, the residual variance was increased an average of 5–10 percent for all fitted equations. It is concluded from this analysis that market interest rates introduce additional risk or uncertainty into the warrant pricing process. The next chapter will discuss the effects of interest rate risk in greater detail.

attempts to relate warrant price changes to the price-making activity of speculative markets.

2. The fundamental equations fitted above offer a theory of expectations which rests on the premise that all warrant price changes are formed according to anticipated stock price. [In this regard, see Chapter 2.] Here the behavior of warrant investors provides the motivation for price changes. Warrant investors are speculators who desire quick profits. As such, they constantly seek information that enables them to predict what average opinion believes to be reasonable focus values. Warrants that are unaffected by market focus outcomes will return the riskless rate, while those which move with market focus outcomes will promise an appropriately higher expected return.

The basic idea of these results parallels the model of Working (1958). He concludes that prices must be formed under the influence of expectations. In Working's scheme, traders must constantly search for new information which permits them to predict price changes. But the information on which future events are based is itself unpredictable. Consequently, it is the random quality of new information which is responsible for unpredictable price changes.

The equations are also consistent with the theory of efficient markets expounded by Sharpe (1964), Fama (1970), and others. An efficient market is an idealized market that assumes that (1) there are no transaction costs, (2) every trader acts rationally, and (3) all important current information is freely available. In an efficient market, current prices "fully reflect" all available information. Within this context, the results of this chapter suggest that the adjustment of actual warrant prices precedes the events which are the basis of the change. In other words, actual warrant prices "fully reflect" events which the market expects to take place in the future.

3. Among the essential characteristics of expectations is the range of investor perception. Sprenkle (1961) suggests that the horizon of investors in the warrant market is not too far. The empirical results above indicate that if one wants to explain warrant price changes over a month, it is important to know what the market thinks focus outcomes will be next month.

4. Given the form (5.14), the coefficient $\hat{\beta}_0$ for the focus high models is smaller than the coefficient $\hat{\beta}_1$. For the focus low models, the coefficients $\hat{\beta}_0$ and $\hat{\beta}_1$ are nearly equal. This distinction is readily seen in the table below, which presents the coefficients $\hat{\beta}_0$ and $\hat{\beta}_1$ averaged over all eight warrants.

	$\hat{\beta}_0$	$\hat{\beta}_1$
Focus High Models	.582	.918
Focus Low Models	.732	.618

It is conceivable that this is caused to some extent by the recent history of the stock price. Kassouf (1968) suggests that warrant investors are anti-chartists who believe that recent stock trends are more apt to reverse themselves than continue. If this is true, the magnitude of the coefficients above suggests that warrant investors on the average are interested in warrants whose stocks have fallen because they are due to rise.

It could be, however, that investors treat gains and losses differently due to their economic distinctions. Burrell (1950) offers support for this contention. He implies that investor attitude toward changing market trends will be different depending on the investor's current profit or loss position (measured with respect to his purchase cost).

5. It is worthwhile to comment on the degree of explanation achieved by the individual models. In general, one finds a moderate fit for nearly all the equations. Comparison of the residual variance of these fitted models with the residual variance of the warrant series alone reveals that, for the focus high and low models, the average reduction has been 58.7 percent and 59.0 percent respectively.

6. Despite the innovative theory and methods used, optimism must be tempered with caution for at least three reasons. First, the models developed are not prediction equations, but causal models hypothesized to explain the behavior of warrant price changes in response to expectational stimuli. Formal acceptance of the theoretical considerations of Chapter 2 requires additional empirical testing for different types of options over various periods of time.

Second, it must be admitted that the high and low stock prices are at best error-ridden proxies for the "true" focus outcomes on which warrant investment decisions are "actually" based. This is one of the pitfalls lying between the theoretical and empirical models above, which were formulated on the notion of focus values. Data lacking in quality can hardly be expected to provide adequate coefficients, especially where the measurement errors are known to cause bias. The consequences of using such coefficients are even worse if a greater degree of causality is attributed to the coefficients than they deserve.

Finally, the estimated coefficients can be questioned when specification errors are present. If a relatively important variable is left out of an equation, any measured responses will not only exclude this factor, but the coefficients of the focus values will also be biased. Among the more serious sources of specification error for the fitted fundamental dynamic models is the failure to include various psychological aspects of the stock market. The question of additional exogenous influences will be taken up in the next chapter.

6

DATA ANALYSIS OF THE BEHAVIORAL DYNAMIC EQUATION

Introduction

This chapter summarizes the results of extending the dynamic modeling procedure of Chapter 5 to include several variables, each with a rational lag function. The approach taken to develop a broader theory of price explanation has been to propose a number of possible price determinants. Actual testing of the hypotheses requires evaluating two-stage cross correlation estimates between warrant changes and each of the determinants. In essence, empirical results will be used to develop a structure for explaining warrant pricing.

In building behavioral equations by means of multivariate dynamic models, however, variable interrelationships complicate model identification. Unless a priori patterns are theoretically justifiable, it is difficult in practice to analyze the joint dependence structure. Only in the case of independent inputs is identification tractable.

For these reasons, a principal components analysis is used to specify the original determinants as a parsimonious set of independent variables. To test the influence of these dimensions on price, cross correlation estimates are computed between warrant changes and each of the components. Based on the results of these estimates, behavioral equations can be constructed for each of the warrants by building upon the fundamental dynamic equations of Chapter 5.

Exogenous Influences

Warrant price changes can be said to arise from a number of measurable influences. The investigations of this section, however, will be confined to the determinants selected in Chapter 4.

Price-Exogenous Relationships

It is hypothesized that the following series are related to changes in warrant price: the bond price for bond usable warrants, warrant volume, common volume, warrant volatility, and common volatility. A discussion of these series is given in Chapter 4. Table 14 presents cross correlation estimates for these various relations computed by using the two-stage method. Essentially, the sample cross correlations tell us whether any of the variables for the last ten months or the next ten months are likely to be related to the current warrant price change. Under the assumption of series independence, one can test the validity of these propositions. An examination of the table yields the following conclusions:

1. There is a significant positive relationship at lag $k = 0$ between the warrant pricing process and the size of both warrant volume and common volume. These findings clearly support earlier studies by Hsu (1973) and Leabo and Rogalski (1974a).
2. The estimates do not support the contention that stock price volatility and warrant changes are positively related. Previous studies have not provided definite support for this hypothesis. Van Horne (1969) and Melicher and Rush (1974) found a significant positive relationship, but Shelton (1967) did not.[1]
3. There is some evidence of a significant negative relation between current warrant changes and warrant volatility one month in the future. This provides support for the proposition by Leabo and Rogalski (1974b) that warrant price changes have a tendency to reverse directions over time.
4. The estimated cross correlations at lag $k = 0$ support the hypothesis that interest rate risk associated with bond usable warrants positively influences warrant pricing decisions. An earlier study by Melicher and Rush (1974) suggested this relationship, but their results were statistically inconclusive.

1. One reason for the inconsistency in reported studies is the measure of volatility used. The papers by Van Horne (1968) and Melicher and Rush (1974) defined volatility to be simply the difference between the high and low market prices of the common stock (in specified preceding years) over the average of the high and low for those years.

Another reason could be that these studies dealt with cross sectional data. The only "time series" analysis of warrants in the literature appeared in the same article by Van Horne (1968). Using three perpetual warrants, he again examines the influence of volatility. It is important to note, however, that he changes the measure of volatility to be the ratio of the average market price for the previous eighteen months to the standard deviation about that average price. By doing so, the influence of volatility is at best marginal.

Table 14
PRICE-EXOGENOUS RELATIONSHIPS

Warrant	Lags	0	1	2	3	4	5	6	7	8	9	10
(a) Estimated Cross Correlation Function $r_k[\varepsilon(t:z_1);\varepsilon(t:y_c)]$												
Allegheny Airlines (1987)	0 to 10	.35	−.07	−.06	−.16	−.07	−.11	−.03	.05	−.08	.02	−.12
	−1 to −10		.03	.14	.06	.15	−.04	−.14	.04	.13	−.04	−.04
American Telephone &	0 to 10	.49	−.20	−.17	−.17	−.03	−.09	−.06	−.19	.02	.25	.17
Telegraph	−1 to −10		.18	.07	−.08	−.08	−.25	.30	−.16	−.14	.03	−.26
Avco	0 to 10	.42	−.05	−.09	−.10	.25	−.11	−.25	.11	.03	.03	.17
	−1 to −10		.07	.18	.04	.02	−.08	−.20	−.03	−.03	−.03	−.19
Gulf & Western	0 to 10	.31	.00	−.04	−.13	−.16	−.09	−.09	−.14	−.13	−.01	−.20
	−1 to −10		.08	.11	.08	.00	.02	.05	.12	−.06	−.14	.08
Loews	0 to 10	.17	−.22	.14	−.03	.02	−.08	−.02	−.11	.15	−.06	−.22
	−1 to −10		−.01	.30	.18	.03	.05	.22	.18	.02	.09	.03
Northwest	0 to 10	.47	−.05	.10	−.11	.26	.00	−.05	.15	.09	.09	−.02
	−1 to −10		.02	.14	.05	−.09	−.12	.08	.33	−.09	−.29	−.09
Tenneco	0 to 10	.30	.12	.22	−.07	.14	−.08	−.12	−.02	−.12	−.13	.03
	−1 to −10		−.05	.09	.10	.12	.02	.10	−.06	−.03	.05	.04
Trans World Airlines	0 to 10	−.04	−.01	.02	−.04	.08	−.03	−.05	.19	−.05	.12	.06
	−1 to −10		−.11	.05	−.02	−.13	−.05	.03	.03	.07	.00	.03
(b) Estimated Cross Correlation Function $r_k[\varepsilon(t:z_2);\varepsilon(t:y_c)]$												
Allegheny Airlines (1987)	0 to 10	.42	−.07	−.08	.00	.06	−.19	−.15	.08	−.15	−.12	.03
	−1 to −10		−.02	.06	−.12	.14	.06	−.18	.00	.10	.13	−.13
American Telephone &	0 to 10	.40	−.03	−.16	−.24	−.14	−.16	.22	−.12	.12	.05	.04
Telegraph	−1 to −10		.00	.11	−.03	.08	−.05	.02	−.36	.03	−.14	−.13

(continued)

TABLE 14 *Continued*

WARRANT	LAGS	0	1	2	3	4	5	6	7	8	9	10
Avco	0 to 10	.50	−.06	.00	−.10	.05	.23	−.14	−.04	.18	.27	.03
	−1 to −10		−.07	.17	−.01	−.03	.00	−.22	.03	.13	−.09	−.14
Gulf & Western	0 to 10	.02	.13	.04	−.27	−.11	.11	−.07	−.07	−.02	−.09	−.11
	−1 to −10		−.12	−.04	−.02	−.08	−.01	.06	.00	−.13	−.08	.05
Loews	0 to 10	.01	−.18	.02	−.06	.30	−.17	−.03	.13	.08	.06	−.17
	−1 to −10		.01	.15	.08	.14	.07	.06	.07	.01	−.03	.04
Northwest	0 to 10	.38	−.02	−.04	.06	.12	−.09	−.06	.14	−.05	−.15	−.11
	−1 to −10		.03	.15	.35	.19	.11	.04	.45	.05	−.11	.23
Tenneco	0 to 10	.39	.05	.19	.21	.08	.07	−.18	−.19	.05	−.20	−.05
	−1 to −10		−.19	.04	.11	−.06	.20	−.11	−.02	−.01	−.12	−.12
Trans World Airlines	0 to 10	.13	−.15	.00	.16	−.04	−.05	.06	.07	.03	.07	.00
	−1 to −10		.00	.12	.07	.01	.04	.00	.15	.03	−.03	−.06
(*c*) ESTIMATED CROSS CORRELATION FUNCTION $r_k[\varepsilon(t:z_3);\varepsilon(t:y_c)]$												
Allegheny Airlines (1987)	0 to 10	.17	.14	−.01	.10	−.09	−.08	−.09	−.01	−.01	−.03	.02
	−1 to −10		−.15	−.15	−.14	.10	−.20	−.09	.09	.11	.05	−.07
American Telephone &	0 to 10	.36	.00	.21	−.09	−.05	−.34	.17	−.08	−.05	.18	.09
Telegraph	−1 to −10		−.26	−.12	.09	−.31	.03	.11	−.14	.00	.15	.01
Avco	0 to 10	.28	−.05	−.11	−.05	.01	.10	−.13	−.01	.19	.12	−.18
	−1 to −10		−.55	−.03	−.12	.05	−.18	−.07	.07	.01	−.07	−.06
Gulf & Western	0 to 10	.10	.07	.28	−.07	.16	.08	.05	.27	.17	.14	.01
	−1 to −10		−.41	−.04	−.15	−.21	.00	−.21	−.06	−.11	.01	−.07
Loews	0 to 10	−.03	−.04	.12	−.01	.32	−.05	.14	.05	.23	.01	.10
	−1 to −10		−.48	−.05	−.01	−.26	−.04	−.05	.15	−.10	.14	−.27
Northwest	0 to 10	−.17	−.23	.38	.05	−.13	−.10	−.08	.11	.18	.25	.13
	−1 to −10		−.01	.00	.02	−.01	−.01	−.01	−.01	−.02	−.02	−.02

Tenneco	0 to 10	.09	.01	.20	.06	.14	−.20	−.03	−.15	−.20	−.04	.16
	−1 to −10		−.26	.05	−.01	−.09	.12	.13	.06	.14	−.02	.04
Trans World Airlines	0 to 10	−.07	−.12	−.09	.00	.01	−.05	−.05	.02	.00	−.01	−.20
	−1 to −10		−.28	.00	.04	−.09	−.10	.00	−.05	.01	−.06	−.14

(*d*) Estimated Cross Correlation Function $r_k[\varepsilon(t:z_4);\varepsilon(t:y_c)]$

Allegheny Airlines (1987)	0 to 10	.15	.08	.15	.10	−.10	−.04	−.10	−.03	−.16	.05	−.11
	−1 to −10		−.12	.08	−.16	−.03	−.11	−.01	.04	.12	.00	−.09
American Telephone &	0 to 10	.25	.26	.01	−.19	.17	−.21	−.16	−.06	−.17	−.02	.27
Telegraph	−1 to −10		.25	−.02	.02	−.22	−.08	.02	−.12	−.06	.07	.03
Avco	0 to 10	.11	.01	.10	−.02	.28	.21	.11	.00	.29	.30	−.09
	−1 to −10		−.27	.19	−.04	−.15	−.13	−.09	.08	−.06	−.08	−.10
Gulf & Western	0 to 10	.10	−.12	−.03	−.14	.03	−.07	−.06	.23	.12	.12	−.05
	−1 to −10		−.43	−.17	−.17	−.13	−.06	−.13	.03	−.08	−.11	−.03
Loews	0 to 10	−.13	.04	−.08	.21	.15	−.16	.11	.02	.21	.07	.26
	−1 to −10		.05	−.22	.18	−.30	−.26	−.06	.08	−.01	−.09	−.11
Northwest	0 to 10	−.19	−.05	−.09	−.13	.20	−.09	−.19	−.06	.03	−.01	−.09
	−1 to −10		−.39	−.07	.17	−.31	−.06	.10	.08	−.09	−.23	.18
Tenneco	0 to 10	.03	.06	.18	.01	.35	−.05	.21	−.02	.27	−.18	.11
	−1 to −10		−.24	−.06	−.07	−.12	.06	−.03	.22	−.04	.02	.01
Trans World Airlines	0 to 10	−.10	.02	.07	.00	.18	−.09	.13	.18	−.01	.05	.01
	−1 to −10		−.18	−.08	.17	.01	−.16	−.02	−.10	.05	.01	−.12

(*e*) Estimated Cross Correlation Function $r_k[\varepsilon(t:z_5);\varepsilon(t:y_c)]$

Allegheny Airlines (1987)	0 to 10	.41	−.04	.02	.09	.08	−.12	−.09	.11	−.04	−.08	.01
	−1 to −10		.05	.03	.06	−.08	.15	−.17	−.14	−.17	.16	.10
Avco	0 to 10	.57	.28	−.07	.03	.06	.06	−.30	.06	−.12	−.28	.04
	−1 to −10		.09	.06	.00	.15	−.07	.01	.04	−.10	−.23	.20

(continued)

TABLE 14 *Continued*

WARRANT	LAGS	0	1	2	3	4	5	6	7	8	9	10
Loews	0 to 10	.43	−.01	.03	.08	.08	−.02	.14	.03	−.16	.02	−.08
	−1 to −10		.06	.20	.08	.13	−.01	.10	−.15	−.25	.01	.19
Northwest	0 to 10	.56	.11	.15	−.23	−.06	.05	.07	.04	−.03	−.10	.02
	−1 to −10		.01	−.18	.06	.12	.34	.14	−.14	−.01	−.01	.11
Tenneco	0 to 10	.26	.00	.04	.00	.05	.23	−.23	.01	−.16	−.11	−.13
	−1 to −10		−.07	.03	.10	.00	−.09	.20	−.11	−.03	.07	−.01
Trans World Airlines	0 to 10	.45	.20	−.03	.01	.08	.06	.08	.04	−.03	.05	.01
	−1 to −10		.10	.05	−.10	.14	.06	.00	.12	−.06	.07	.05

Additional investigations were made to examine for dependence between the focus values and each of the determinants. Although the results are not reported, some reasonable conclusions were obtained:

1. Focus high changes are positively (and significantly) related to warrant volume and common volume but are not related to warrant volatility or common volatility.
2. There is some indication that focus low changes may be negatively (and significantly) related to warrant volume or common volume.
3. Changes for both focus values are positively (and significantly) related to bond price changes.

Exogenous Interrelationships

One of the objectives of this study is to identify market interrelationships. Therefore, it is desired to test various combinations of the exogenous variables for dependence by using the two-stage method under the assumption of series independence. Cross correlations have been estimated for all combinations of the determinants and appear in Table 15. From this table one can observe the following:

1. Significant positive relationships between warrant volume and common volume were found at lag $k = 0$.
2. The data support the contention that warrant volatility and common volatility are significantly and positively related at lag $k = 0$.
3. There is some evidence that at lag $k = 0$ warrant volatility and common volatility are significantly and positively related to common volume. This agrees with Douglas's (1969) earlier finding of a positive coefficient between volatility and volume.
4. For bond usable warrants, the bond price is not related over time to warrant volume, common volume, warrant volatility, or common volatility. Hence, there is some evidence that the factors considered are distinct from money market rates.

Principal Components

Evidence has been introduced above to suggest that the exogenous variables considered are highly interrelated at lag $k = 0$. The purpose of this section is to determine any hidden factors which may have generated this joint dependence structure.

Principal components analysis is a procedure developed for the

TABLE 15
EXOGENOUS INTERRELATIONSHIPS

WARRANT	LAGS	0	1	2	3	4	5	6	7	8	9	10
(a) ESTIMATED CROSS CORRELATION FUNCTION $r_k[\varepsilon(t:z_2);\ \varepsilon(t:z_1)]$												
Allegheny Airlines (1987)	0 to 10	.64	−.02	.02	.33	.05	−.15	.09	−.07	−.14	−.06	−.09
	−1 to −10		−.03	.13	.00	−.01	.00	−.01	−.02	−.08	.08	−.13
American Telephone &	0 to 10	.54	.18	.07	−.01	−.06	−.20	.30	.14	.08	.05	−.04
Telegraph	−1 to −10		−.35	.19	−.08	.03	.03	−.21	−.21	−.11	−.14	.16
Avco	0 to 10	.47	.30	−.08	−.12	.14	.10	−.19	−.02	−.11	.25	−.04
	−1 to −10		−.18	.13	−.13	−.05	−.01	−.02	−.05	−.04	.11	−.05
Gulf & Western	0 to 10	.15	.00	−.04	−.12	.16	−.06	.02	.18	.12	−.03	−.08
	−1 to −10		−.07	.01	.10	.03	−.06	.21	.20	−.21	−.08	.09
Loews	0 to 10	.40	−.02	−.06	.11	.05	.12	.03	.02	−.02	.10	.16
	−1 to −10		−.14	−.10	−.07	.03	−.01	−.14	−.07	−.02	.01	.08
Northwest	0 to 10	.49	−.18	−.24	.04	.02	−.18	−.15	.15	−.16	−.10	.02
	−1 to −10		.05	−.04	.12	.31	.06	−.11	.19	−.13	.05	.12
Tenneco	0 to 10	.48	.11	.15	.11	.03	.01	.11	−.01	.02	.09	−.19
	−1 to −10		−.01	.17	−.04	−.12	−.05	−.16	.16	−.12	.06	−.06
Trans World Airlines	0 to 10	.28	.07	.13	−.09	−.14	.14	.00	.04	−.06	.07	−.01
	−1 to −10		.21	−.16	−.18	.02	.04	.05	.07	−.08	−.05	−.06
(b) ESTIMATED CROSS CORRELATION FUNCTION $r_k[\varepsilon(t:z_3);\ \varepsilon(t:z_1)]$												
Allegheny Airlines (1987)	0 to 10	.26	−.07	−.06	−.06	.03	.03	.01	−.10	−.12	−.05	−.01
	−1 to −10		.03	.10	−.09	.05	−.19	.03	.03	.01	−.09	−.03
American Telephone &	0 to 10	.27	.11	−.02	.20	.01	−.35	.22	−.18	−.05	−.08	.10
Telegraph	−1 to −10		−.14	.23	.15	−.10	.10	.03	.07	.26	.20	.23
Avco	0 to 10	.27	.03	−.10	.07	.05	.03	−.14	.00	.00	.23	−.14
	−1 to −10		−.36	−.03	−.05	.06	−.15	−.01	.21	−.11	−.05	−.02

Gulf & Western	0 to 10	.26	−.16	−.12	−.21	.01	.05	−.25	.02	.22	.12	.05
	−1 to −10		−.22	−.33	−.01	−.11	.11	−.13	−.19	.07	.02	.04
Loews	0 to 10	.12	−.22	−.20	−.13	.05	−.17	−.02	−.04	.01	−.01	.34
	−1 to −10		−.22	−.14	−.03	−.14	.06	−.22	.04	−.06	−.15	−.07
Northwest	0 to 10	.07	−.16	.11	−.08	.07	−.07	−.16	−.04	.01	.34	.07
	−1 to −10		.00	.00	.00	.00	.01	.00	.01	.00	.00	.00
Tenneco	0 to 10	.34	.07	−.05	−.03	−.04	−.12	−.10	.07	−.03	−.10	.01
	−1 to −10		−.09	.05	.06	−.01	−.15	.14	−.09	.13	.16	−.29
Trans World Airlines	0 to 10	.06	.04	.19	.11	.10	−.09	−.11	.10	.00	.05	−.07
	−1 to −10		.06	−.08	.03	.04	−.01	.03	.02	−.01	.00	−.04

(c) ESTIMATED CROSS CORRELATION FUNCTION $r_k[\varepsilon(t:z_3);\varepsilon(t:z_2)]$

Allegheny Airlines (1987)	0 to 10	.33	.00	−.05	.15	−.10	.08	−.12	−.10	.05	.04	−.13
	−1 to −10		.04	.10	.03	.16	−.16	.04	.11	−.13	.03	.07
American Telephone &	0 to 10	.24	−.13	−.01	.17	−.23	−.08	.02	−.36	.05	−.21	.16
Telegraph	−1 to −10		−.37	−.03	.11	−.07	.04	.26	−.12	.31	.15	.15
Avco	0 to 10	.41	−.08	.10	.10	−.08	.05	−.09	−.02	.07	.12	−.19
	−1 to −10		−.29	−.06	−.17	.21	.00	−.15	−.01	−.10	.01	−.21
Gulf & Western	0 to 10	.24	−.02	−.05	.02	−.02	−.09	.08	.04	−.06	−.03	−.04
	−1 to −10		−.16	−.25	−.04	.16	−.04	−.06	.06	−.05	.05	.02
Loews	0 to 10	.20	−.20	−.19	−.09	.05	−.05	−.10	.07	.06	−.01	.08
	−1 to −10		−.06	.01	.01	−.05	−.13	−.02	−.09	−.22	−.14	.02
Northwest	0 to 10	.09	−.13	.07	−.19	−.05	−.06	.11	−.16	−.08	.15	.21
	−1 to −10		−.02	−.03	−.01	−.03	−.02	−.03	−.02	−.03	−.03	−.03
Tenneco	0 to 10	.25	.08	.00	−.13	−.41	−.11	.04	.08	−.06	−.05	.06
	−1 to −10		.00	.12	−.01	−.13	.08	.14	−.05	.19	.01	−.06
Trans World Airlines	0 to 10	.32	.04	.06	.02	−.08	.00	−.10	−.13	.08	.01	−.16
	−1 to −10		−.09	.00	−.08	.04	−.02	−.05	−.08	−.02	.00	.02

(continued)

TABLE 15 *Continued*

WARRANT	LAGS	0	1	2	3	4	5	6	7	8	9	10
(*d*) ESTIMATED CROSS CORRELATION FUNCTION $r_k[\varepsilon(t:z_3);\ \varepsilon(t:z_5)]$												
Allegheny Airlines (1987)	0 to 10	−.04	.14	−.03	.07	−.17	−.16	.12	.09	.22	−.12	.11
	−1 to −10		.04	−.21	−.04	.13	−.02	.08	−.09	−.09	−.21	.01
Avco	0 to 10	.10	−.20	−.15	−.22	.17	−.05	−.03	.01	.25	−.05	−.15
	−1 to −10		−.17	−.11	−.01	.03	−.05	−.26	.11	−.10	.07	.16
Loews	0 to 10	−.29	−.09	.16	−.05	.13	−.01	.29	.12	.23	.01	−.10
	−1 to −10		−.42	.05	.13	−.31	.07	−.08	−.12	−.23	.10	−.15
Northwest	0 to 10	.09	−.20	.30	.05	−.34	−.26	−.23	.30	.26	.02	−.07
	−1 to −10		−.03	.00	−.01	−.02	−.01	−.02	−.01	−.02	−.02	−.01
Tenneco	0 to 10	−.11	.02	−.01	.13	−.12	−.20	−.12	.05	−.01	.10	.08
	−1 to −10		−.14	.21	.13	.13	−.26	−.18	.04	.19	−.21	.35
Trans World Airlines	0 to 10	−.10	−.02	−.01	−.02	.09	.05	.02	−.03	−.06	−.01	−.16
	−1 to −10		−.16	−.15	.12	.07	.00	−.01	.01	.00	−.05	−.04
(*e*) ESTIMATED CROSS CORRELATION FUNCTION $r_k[\varepsilon(t:z_4);\ \varepsilon(t:z_1)]$												
Allegheny Airlines (1987)	0 to 10	.21	−.06	.01	.15	.06	.07	−.01	−.12	−.06	−.06	−.11
	−1 to −10		−.01	.11	−.14	−.07	−.06	.03	.01	−.02	−.03	−.13
American Telephone & Telegraph	0 to 10	.26	.00	−.01	.02	−.05	−.05	−.07	−.30	−.13	−.36	.17
	−1 to −10		−.07	−.07	−.05	−.16	.01	−.09	−.14	.18	−.06	.35
Avco	0 to 10	.25	.07	.06	−.03	.14	.10	−.02	.04	.00	.14	−.10
	−1 to −10		−.04	.00	−.18	.11	−.03	.03	.16	−.27	.05	−.01
Gulf & Western	0 to 10	.32	−.09	−.17	−.20	.08	−.09	−.21	.01	.09	.05	.04
	−1 to −10		−.11	−.16	−.08	.01	.10	.07	−.13	.09	.18	.17
Loews	0 to 10	−.04	−.10	−.18	−.12	−.09	−.03	−.03	−.09	−.07	.01	.23
	−1 to −10		.11	−.28	−.08	−.17	.29	−.21	−.08	−.04	.05	−.02

Northwest	0 to 10	.26	−.23	−.13	−.19	.22	−.07	−.22	−.06	.10	.10	.00
	−1 to −10		−.17	−.25	.11	.04	.10	.06	.06	−.09	−.10	.09
Tenneco	0 to 10	.13	−.08	.07	.17	.31	.10	.33	.18	.22	−.15	.20
	−1 to −10		.01	−.17	−.03	.04	−.12	−.14	.10	−.02	−.02	−.16
Trans World Airlines	0 to 10	.10	−.08	.20	−.01	.14	−.07	−.08	−.04	.05	.02	.00
	−1 to −10		.07	.04	−.04	−.04	−.02	−.11	.01	−.08	.18	−.10
(f) ESTIMATED CROSS CORRELATION FUNCTION $r_k[\varepsilon(t: z_4); \varepsilon(t: z_2)]$												
Allegheny Airlines (1987)	0 to 10	.36	−.07	.12	.08	−.04	.07	−.06	−.10	−.05	.08	−.20
	−1 to −10		.07	−.01	.02	−.03	−.21	.04	−.05	−.02	.01	−.13
American Telephone &	0 to 10	.04	−.09	.05	.01	−.19	.06	−.25	−.15	−.12	−.18	.29
Telegraph	−1 to −10		−.15	−.13	−.07	−.16	−.09	−.09	−.05	.22	−.07	.06
Avco	0 to 10	.40	−.05	.07	−.01	.16	.04	.01	−.12	.02	.15	−.24
	−1 to −10		.15	.24	−.07	.07	.25	−.04	.16	−.09	−.06	.01
Gulf & Western	0 to 10	.24	−.04	−.03	.07	.04	−.08	.11	.04	−.02	−.04	.04
	−1 to −10		.05	−.15	−.07	.13	−.03	.08	.06	.03	−.01	−.03
Loews	0 to 10	.01	−.22	−.21	−.09	−.05	.09	−.08	.00	.00	.00	.05
	−1 to −10		.03	−.24	−.12	−.18	.18	−.35	−.31	−.04	−.30	.18
Northwest	0 to 10	.20	−.01	−.27	−.39	.14	−.05	−.29	−.07	−.06	.07	−.07
	−1 to −10		−.21	−.29	.31	−.14	.10	−.02	.04	−.04	−.05	.12
Tenneco	0 to 10	.19	−.06	.05	.04	.05	.29	.31	.08	−.01	−.18	.14
	−1 to −10		−.14	.03	−.14	−.22	−.06	−.09	.22	−.10	.18	.11
Trans World Airlines	0 to 10	.26	.02	.04	−.02	.02	.00	−.04	−.05	.04	.03	−.05
	−1 to −10		−.06	.03	.14	−.02	−.03	.01	.00	−.15	.12	.02
(g) ESTIMATED CROSS CORRELATION FUNCTION $r_k[\varepsilon(t: z_4); \varepsilon(t: z_3)]$												
Allegheny Airlines (1987)	0 to 10	.61	.15	.06	−.12	−.10	−.11	.19	−.09	−.13	−.08	−.05
	−1 to −10		.04	−.04	−.18	.01	−.11	.15	−.06	−.18	.10	−.17
American Telephone &	0 to 10	.40	−.19	.07	−.21	.00	.01	−.10	−.03	−.19	−.06	.04
Telegraph	−1 to −10		.07	.05	.12	−.23	.12	−.03	.05	.11	.11	−.09

(continued)

TABLE 15 *Continued*

WARRANT	LAGS	0	1	2	3	4	5	6	7	8	9	10
Avco	0 to 10	.34	−.14	.07	−.02	.13	−.27	−.11	−.25	.18	.05	−.29
	−1 to −10		−.03	.08	.11	.09	.04	−.09	.24	.03	−.03	−.01
Gulf & Western	0 to 10	.71	−.07	−.02	.12	.12	.14	−.11	.00	.02	.25	.05
	−1 to −10		.07	−.09	−.22	−.08	.02	−.15	−.20	−.07	.19	−.03
Loews	0 to 10	.34	.18	.10	−.04	−.02	.07	.51	−.04	.08	.02	.14
	−1 to −10		.32	.02	.07	.21	.16	−.11	.03	.14	.09	−.04
Northwest	0 to 10	.20	.00	.00	−.01	.01	.01	.02	.02	.02	.01	.01
	−1 to −10		−.15	−.06	−.16	−.03	.36	−.14	−.08	−.07	.05	−.29
Tenneco	0 to 10	.25	−.25	−.13	−.17	.16	.07	.02	−.12	−.01	−.12	.07
	−1 to −10		.07	.05	−.31	.07	−.13	.03	−.07	.19	−.04	.10
Trans World Airlines	0 to 10	.55	−.06	.02	−.14	−.02	.06	.00	.01	−.09	.03	.02
	−1 to −10		.04	−.16	.13	.02	.18	−.09	.06	−.06	.05	−.07
(*h*) ESTIMATED CROSS CORRELATION FUNCTION $r_k[\varepsilon(t:z_4);\ \varepsilon(t:z_5)]$												
Allegheny Airlines (1987)	0 to 10	.00	.21	.15	.04	−.28	−.06	−.08	.15	.06	−.01	−.22
	−1 to −10		−.06	−.13	−.05	.03	.07	.03	−.17	−.05	−.26	.14
Avco	0 to 10	.04	−.01	.07	−.05	.24	.06	.03	.10	.38	.04	.04
	−1 to −10		−.02	.02	−.04	−.25	−.07	−.05	.06	−.09	.01	−.05
Loews	0 to 10	−.11	−.07	−.16	.27	.16	−.11	−.11	.08	.26	−.01	.00
	−1 to −10		−.20	−.18	.14	−.16	−.13	−.13	.02	−.18	−.21	−.02
Northwest	0 to 10	−.03	−.37	.01	.00	−.02	−.07	−.04	.03	.02	.07	−.10
	−1 to −10		−.35	.04	.01	−.14	.13	.13	.21	−.13	−.10	.15
Tenneco	0 to 10	−.26	.24	.03	.37	.02	−.01	.14	.15	.09	.00	.00
	−1 to −10		−.08	−.29	.12	−.01	−.06	−.13	−.02	−.08	−.11	.03
Trans World Airlines	0 to 10	−.13	.14	.02	.10	.06	−.02	.21	−.08	.10	−.01	.10
	−1 to −10		−.25	−.03	.15	.16	−.10	−.04	−.01	.03	.00	−.01

(*i*) Estimated Cross Correlation Function $r_k[\varepsilon(t: z_5); \varepsilon(t: z_1)]$

Allegheny Airlines (1987)	0 to 10	−.02	−.04	.13	.20	.10	−.06	.02	−.01	−.09	.00	.10
	−1 to −10		−.02	.00	−.01	−.14	−.11	−.06	−.09	.03	.17	−.06
Avco	0 to 10	.32	.24	.00	.18	.13	.03	−.33	.02	−.13	−.24	−.07
	−1 to −10		−.17	−.12	.05	.16	−.24	−.04	−.05	.17	−.05	.20
Loews	0 to 10	.07	.00	.25	.12	.08	.05	.22	.24	.03	.06	−.14
	−1 to −10		−.18	.02	−.07	−.01	.15	−.09	−.25	.22	.19	−.21
Northwest	0 to 10	.27	.08	.46	.09	−.07	−.14	.05	.13	−.11	−.11	−.28
	−1 to −10		−.14	−.05	−.04	.05	.04	−.14	−.10	.02	.17	.02
Tenneco	0 to 10	.25	−.07	.12	.13	.21	−.05	−.11	.01	−.12	.00	−.09
	−1 to −10		.21	.13	−.08	.02	.03	−.04	−.06	.03	.15	.17
Trans World Airlines	0 to 10	.15	−.05	−.02	.13	−.08	−.05	−.04	.10	.08	.11	−.10
	−1 to −10		.15	−.02	.13	.13	−.09	.04	.05	.11	.12	.07

(*j*) Estimated Cross Correlation Function $r_k[\varepsilon(t: z_5); \varepsilon(t: z_2)]$

Allegheny Airlines (1987)	0 to 10	.20	−.08	.08	.16	.15	−.09	.00	.04	−.05	.11	.02
	−1 to −10		.12	−.15	.11	−.10	.00	−.14	−.05	−.03	.10	.04
Avco	0 to 10	.23	.09	.02	.08	.02	.06	−.13	.03	−.15	−.12	.03
	−1 to −10		.00	.10	−.12	.20	.09	−.13	−.08	.23	.21	.12
Loews	0 to 10	.08	.00	.27	.11	.01	.12	.05	.04	−.01	−.07	.03
	−1 to −10		.04	−.01	.14	−.12	.09	.08	.01	.29	.15	−.22
Northwest	0 to 10	.19	−.07	.36	.09	.09	.05	.07	.35	−.19	−.11	.04
	−1 to −10		.06	.03	.13	−.16	.19	−.04	.05	−.02	.05	.06
Tenneco	0 to 10	.16	−.10	.24	.04	.06	.03	−.27	−.10	−.09	.22	.05
	−1 to −10		.25	.05	.17	−.01	−.18	−.03	−.24	.04	.15	.07
Trans World Airlines	0 to 10	−.02	−.01	−.08	.12	−.05	.08	.02	.03	.02	−.05	−.06
	−1 to −10		−.11	−.06	.25	.06	−.03	.01	−.01	.09	.06	.03

purpose of analyzing intercorrelations at lag $k = 0$ within a set of variables. This technique is generally useful whenever the task is to determine the smallest number of independent dimensions needed to account for most of the variance in the original set of variables. That is, the original symmetric variables are represented as functions of latent factor variables. The analysis of the dependence structure at lag $k = 0$ amounts to statistical estimation of the coefficients of the functions, termed *components*. If the first few components account for most of the total variance, and if these dimensions can be interpreted meaningfully, the original set of exogenous variables can be described more parsimoniously by them. The resulting pairs of components are in principle uncorrelated at lag $k = 0$.

After orthogonally transforming the original variables to a set of principal components, investor perceptions of market information might be viewed as investors' ability to discriminate between a finite number of dimensions of variation. For example, if warrant investors do distinguish between components of the "market," one would expect that each component would appear as a separate dimension.

Results of Principal Components Analysis

Correlation coefficients of the first three principal components formed from the variables—warrant volume, common volume, warrant volatility, and common volatility—are shown for each warrant in Table 16.[2] It was decided to exclude bond price from the analysis so that (1) components could be compared for all warrants, and (2) because the results of the section on exogenous relationships in this chapter indicate that bond price is independent of the other variables.[3]

The first component appears to be a *general psychological market factor* (PMF) because all exogenous variables have nearly equally high positive correlation with this dimension. Market fluctuations are generally associated with trade volume and price variability. These fluctuations may be generated by investors' psychological perceptions of unobservable exogenous influences, such as political or war news. Roughly half the total variance in the four original dimensions is accounted for by component one.

Component two explained about 25 percent of the total variance. This dimension may be thought of as a *comparison of volume with volatility*.

2. When facing a practical problem in data reduction, one would probably stop with the first two or three components because no parsimony is gained by merely making an orthogonal transformation to four new dimensions.

3. Principal components were formed for various combinations of variables (including both the senior security and the focus values). None was found to have the general interpretation that can be attached to those in Table 16.

Table 16
CORRELATION COEFFICIENTS OF THE PRINCIPAL COMPONENTS

Warrant	Allegheny Airlines (1987)			American Telephone & Telegraph			Avco			Gulf & Western		
Dimension	1	2	3	1	2	3	1	2	3	1	2	3
Warrant Volume	.48	−.57	.30	.58	−.32	.39	.48	.72	.08	.39	.15	.91
Common Volume	.53	−.41	−.35	.50	−.56	−.16	.56	.17	.05	.34	−.94	.01
Warrant Volatility	.50	.49	.68	.49	.41	−.74	.48	−.38	−.76	.60	.21	−.34
Common Volatility	.49	.51	−.59	.41	.64	.53	.47	−.55	.64	.61	.22	−.25
Latent Root (variance)	2.20	1.05	.41	1.89	1.09	.62	2.08	.78	.66	2.03	.86	.82
Percent of Total Variance	55.07	26.27	10.30	47.23	27.28	15.52	51.93	19.43	16.58	50.69	21.61	20.42
Cumulative Percent of Variance	55.07	81.34	91.64	47.23	74.51	90.03	51.93	71.36	87.94	50.67	72.28	92.70
	Loews			Northwest			Tenneco			Trans World Airlines		
Warrant Volume	.52	−.46	−.50	.60	−.33	.07	.57	−.39	.01	.26	.81	.51
Common Volume	.59	−.35	.24	.59	−.32	.31	.55	−.34	−.26	.49	.35	−.78
Warrant Volatility	.53	.44	.58	.27	.81	.52	.50	.25	.79	.59	−.34	.08
Common Volatility	.31	.68	−.60	.45	.37	−.79	.35	.82	−.42	.58	−.32	.35
Latent Root (variance)	1.54	1.24	.63	1.70	1.03	.77	1.83	.94	.73	1.83	1.05	.68
Percent of Total Variance	38.58	31.03	15.83	42.51	25.66	29.19	45.95	23.43	18.32	45.83	26.15	17.02
Cumulative Percent of Variance	38.58	69.61	85.44	42.51	68.17	87.36	45.95	69.38	87.70	45.83	71.98	89.00

For this dimension, volume and volatility have coefficients of opposite signs except for Gulf and Western, where the dimension is clearly dominated by a negative coefficient for common volume.

The third component explains a still smaller proportion of the total variance. This dimension may be thought of as a *comparison of warrant volatility and common volatility*. An exception is Gulf and Western, where the third dimension is highly correlated with warrant volume. For Trans World Airlines the dimension appears to be a comparison of warrant volume and common volume.

Estimated Autocorrelation Functions of the Principal Components

The sample autocorrelation function[4] for each of the principal components is shown in Table 17. Under the null hypothesis of white noise, the autocorrelations should be approximately normally distributed around zero, with standard errors approximately $N^{-1/2}$. Inspection of two standard error limits and comparison of the statistic Q (not shown) with tabulated values of χ^2 do not in general contradict the hypothesis that the components are white noise. This is reasonable because the principal components are simply linear combinations of the original white noise series.

Independence of Principal Components

The hypothesis to be tested in this section is whether the principal components are independent over time. To accomplish this, one can calculate the various cross correlation functions between the white noise components. Under the assumption of series independence, the individual estimates may be judged against an approximate standard error of $N^{-1/2}$.

The estimated cross correlations between the first and second, the first and third, and the second and third principal components are shown in Table 18. From examining this table it appears that an assumption of series independence cannot be rejected. Note that the principal components analysis has produced orthogonal dimensions at lag $k = 0$.

Relationships Between Warrants and Principal Components

Cross correlation estimates have been computed between each principal component and the price series of each warrant. These are tabulated

4. The data have been standardized before forming the linear combination to compute the principal components. Each of the first three components will be symbolically represented over time t as $P_1(t)$, $P_2(t)$, and $P_3(t)$ respectively.

TABLE 17
ESTIMATED AUTOCORRELATIONS OF THE PRINCIPAL COMPONENTS

SERIES	1	2	3	4	5	6	7	8	9	10
				ALLEGHENY AIRLINES (1987)						
P_1	.01	.09	.05	−.02	−.11	.05	−.06	−.12	.00	−.17
P_2	.06	.04	−.06	−.08	−.05	.19	.04	−.14	.01	.01
P_3	−.12	.03	−.07	−.11	.00	−.28	.13	.04	.02	.01
				AMERICAN TELEPHONE & TELEGRAPH						
P_1	−.16	.11	.06	−.20	−.04	.09	−.21	.08	−.09	.20
P_2	.08	.16	−.07	.08	.14	.09	.10	−.16	.15	−.27
P_3	−.06	.01	.04	−.01	.18	.18	−.20	.02	−.10	.01
				AVCO						
P_1	−.08	.06	−.07	.16	.04	−.11	.04	−.07	.15	−.21
P_2	.01	−.03	.14	−.04	−.19	−.02	−.22	.16	−.12	−.05
P_3	.14	−.01	−.14	.03	.28	.17	.13	−.23	−.05	.00
				GULF & WESTERN						
P_1	−.07	−.18	−.08	.07	.04	−.11	−.07	.04	.18	.04
P_2	.05	−.13	−.03	.10	.09	−.13	−.09	.04	.04	−.02
P_3	.12	.14	.25	−.05	.01	.11	−.06	−.08	−.08	−.06
				LOEWS						
P_1	−.15	−.20	−.03	.03	.12	−.11	−.07	−.04	−.04	.21
P_2	.15	.07	.19	.32	.11	.04	.15	.14	−.03	−.01
P_3	−.03	.11	.08	.12	.12	−.03	.09	−.14	.18	−.05
				NORTHWEST						
P_1	−.15	.02	.00	.21	−.01	−.23	.13	−.11	.04	−.09
P_2	.10	.03	.09	.06	.14	−.03	.13	−.01	−.09	−.13
P_3	.11	.18	.15	.06	−.24	.09	.05	.07	.03	.19
				TENNECO						
P_1	−.04	.11	−.02	−.09	.00	.07	.07	.06	−.02	−.07
P_2	.07	.19	−.18	.12	−.08	−.09	−.21	−.06	−.06	−.08
P_3	−.12	.07	.23	−.01	.13	.01	.06	−.09	.04	.03
				TRANS WORLD AIRLINES						
P_1	.00	.01	.00	.00	.07	−.06	−.02	−.06	.05	−.03
P_2	.12	−.12	−.08	−.09	.19	.17	.14	−.10	−.11	.03
P_3	−.04	.06	.13	.03	−.09	.02	−.06	.05	−.18	.02

in Table 19. An examination of the estimates $r_k[\varepsilon(t:P_1); \varepsilon(t:y_c)]$ reveals the occurrence of significant lags at $k = 0$ or $k = -1$. Except for Avco and Northwest, there is little evidence that the second component influences

TABLE 18
PRINCIPAL COMPONENT INTERRELATIONSHIPS

WARRANT	LAGS	0	1	2	3	4	5	6	7	8	9	10
	(*a*) ESTIMATED CROSS CORRELATION FUNCTION $r_k[\varepsilon(t:P_1); \varepsilon(t:P_2)]$											
Allegheny Airlines (1987)	0 to 10	.00	.15	.03	−.31	−.04	−.13	.12	.13	−.05	−.02	.06
	−1 to −10		.05	−.06	−.09	−.08	.13	−.02	−.05	−.05	.01	−.04
American Telephone &	0 to 10	.00	−.03	−.03	.01	−.07	.13	−.04	.14	.23	.21	.03
Telegraph	−1 to −10		.09	.01	.05	−.03	.02	−.18	−.14	−.24	−.17	.06
Avco	0 to 10	.00	.14	−.13	.07	−.06	−.01	−.07	−.17	.05	.24	.01
	−1 to −10		−.17	−.06	−.13	−.08	−.10	.02	.09	−.19	−.04	.19
Gulf & Western	0 to 10	.00	.01	−.02	−.12	−.03	.13	−.22	−.15	.14	.17	.00
	−1 to −10		.01	.15	.05	−.20	.08	−.08	−.17	.00	.10	.07
Loews	0 to 10	.00	.25	.02	−.03	−.05	.14	−.12	−.02	−.03	−.09	−.10
	−1 to −10		.02	−.01	−.11	.10	−.07	.20	.11	.08	.10	.15
Northwest	0 to 10	.00	−.01	−.03	.11	−.18	.10	.12	−.07	.04	−.06	−.05
	−1 to −10		−.12	.09	−.32	−.03	.04	−.07	−.24	.06	.26	−.06
Tenneco	0 to 10	.00	−.07	−.06	−.25	.04	−.15	−.04	−.03	.05	.06	.03
	−1 to −10		−.09	−.04	−.09	.23	.11	.27	.00	.06	−.25	.30
Trans World Airlines	0 to 10	.00	.08	.22	−.01	.02	−.06	−.03	.03	.05	−.02	−.05
	−1 to −10		.12	−.04	−.02	−.02	−.05	.09	.00	−.06	−.08	.09
	(*b*) ESTIMATED CROSS CORRELATION FUNCTION $r_k[\varepsilon(t:P_1); \varepsilon(t:P_3)]$											
Allegheny Airlines (1987)	0 to 10	.00	.11	.05	.02	.15	−.14	.03	−.02	−.01	−.17	.21
	−1 to −10		.05	−.05	−.18	−.01	.00	−.11	−.03	.11	.00	.00
American Telephone &	0 to 10	.00	.34	−.22	−.09	−.08	−.17	−.06	−.12	−.07	−.23	.03
Telegraph	−1 to −10		−.12	.02	−.29	.04	.16	−.32	−.09	−.17	−.18	.28
Avco	0 to 10	.00	.07	.09	.05	−.05	.24	.07	.13	−.09	.00	.14
	−1 to −10		.06	.02	−.11	.12	−.06	.08	−.18	−.02	−.01	−.08

Gulf & Western	0 to 10	.00	−.06	−.05	−.15	.02	−.09	−.13	.10	.17	−.09	.01
	−1 to −10		−.14	−.17	.06	−.07	.05	.11	−.07	.02	−.08	.11
Loews	0 to 10	.00	−.17	.17	−.01	−.04	−.30	.15	.17	−.12	−.08	−.20
	−1 to −10		.06	.05	.04	.15	−.22	−.14	.10	.00	−.01	.02
Northwest	0 to 10	.00	.16	.21	−.18	.15	−.13	−.07	.05	.01	.07	.01
	−1 to −10		−.07	.14	.19	−.12	.10	.13	.08	−.12	.04	.09
Tenneco	0 to 10	.00	−.12	−.04	.10	.11	.02	.22	−.24	.19	.06	−.09
	−1 to −10		.11	−.11	−.15	−.20	−.25	−.11	−.05	−.02	.00	.05
Trans World Airlines	0 to 10	.00	−.09	.08	.10	.09	.07	.00	.11	−.08	.04	.08
	−1 to −10		.09	−.07	−.03	.08	.05	.03	.04	.06	−.09	.01
	(c) Estimated Cross Correlation Function $r_k[\varepsilon(t:P_2);\varepsilon(t:P_3)]$											
Allegheny Airlines (1987)	0 to 10	.00	.11	−.05	.03	−.09	−.01	−.02	−.15	.09	−.07	.03
	−1 to −10		.01	.03	.14	.12	−.04	.03	−.02	.04	−.02	.01
American Telephone &	0 to 10	.00	−.04	.02	.31	.00	.11	.08	−.27	.19	.06	.16
Telegraph	−1 to −10		.02	−.09	.04	.03	−.18	.09	−.28	.06	−.07	.24
Avco	0 to 10	.00	.12	.09	−.14	.00	−.10	−.03	−.22	.03	.12	−.06
	−1 to −10		−.05	.14	−.03	.07	.10	.05	.24	.00	−.07	.17
Gulf & Western	0 to 10	.00	−.09	−.13	.01	−.06	−.01	−.10	−.10	−.06	.00	.09
	−1 to −10		−.01	−.13	−.05	−.08	.04	−.11	−.24	.22	.02	−.05
Loews	0 to 10	.00	.13	−.04	.03	−.11	.16	.14	−.14	−.04	.00	−.07
	−1 to −10		.09	.03	.06	.06	−.06	−.21	−.16	−.12	−.04	−.10
Northwest	0 to 10	.00	−.04	−.07	.07	−.06	−.21	.17	−.01	.01	.00	.30
	−1 to −10		−.04	−.14	−.15	.01	.11	−.10	−.08	−.01	−.06	−.16
Tenneco	0 to 10	.00	−.24	−.24	−.07	.00	.01	−.35	.00	−.12	.02	.07
	−1 to −10		.05	.04	.05	.23	.12	.16	−.15	.30	−.04	.02
Trans World Airlines	0 to 10	.00	−.09	.15	.16	−.09	.01	.05	−.09	.07	−.05	.07
	−1 to −10		−.07	−.01	.10	.20	−.12	.05	.03	.03	−.08	−.03

TABLE 19
RELATIONSHIPS BETWEEN WARRANTS AND PRINCIPAL COMPONENTS

WARRANT	LAGS	0	1	2	3	4	5	6	7	8	9	10
	(*a*) ESTIMATED CROSS CORRELATION FUNCTION $r_k[\varepsilon(t:P_1);\ \varepsilon(t:y_c)]$											
Allegheny Airlines (1987)	0 to 10	.37	.03	.00	.02	−.06	−.14	−.13	.05	−.13	−.03	−.06
	−1 to −10		−.09	.04	−.12	.12	−.09	−.14	.06	.15	.05	−.11
American Telephone &	0 to 10	.56	−.02	−.05	−.25	−.03	−.28	.07	−.17	−.02	.18	.20
Telegraph	−1 to −10		.06	.02	−.01	−.18	−.13	.18	−.29	−.06	.04	−.15
Avco	0 to 10	.47	−.05	−.03	−.10	.20	.16	−.15	.02	.24	.25	−.02
	−1 to −10		−.27	.18	.05	−.04	−.13	−.21	.05	.03	−.10	−.17
Gulf & Western	0 to 10	.18	.01	.10	−.19	.01	.01	−.05	.16	.08	.09	−.10
	−1 to −10		−.36	−.07	−.12	−.16	−.02	−.12	.02	−.13	−.01	−.01
Loews	0 to 10	.03	−.19	.10	.01	.32	−.18	.06	.04	.25	.02	−.07
	−1 to −10		−.19	.12	.16	−.10	−.03	.08	.19	−.03	.06	−.11
Northwest	0 to 10	.29	−.10	.08	−.06	.22	−.09	−.13	.13	.07	.02	−.06
	−1 to −10		−.12	.11	.24	−.07	−.03	.09	.38	−.05	−.27	.12
Tenneco	0 to 10	.33	.09	.29	.08	.23	−.09	−.07	−.14	−.03	−.20	.08
	−1 to −10		−.25	.06	.07	−.03	.15	.03	.06	.03	−.03	−.01
Trans World Airlines	0 to 10	−.03	−.10	−.01	.05	.08	−.08	.04	.15	.00	.07	−.07
	−1 to −10		−.22	.02	.11	−.06	−.11	.00	.00	.05	−.03	−.13
	(*b*) ESTIMATED CROSS CORRELATION FUNCTION $r_k[\varepsilon(t:P_2);\ \varepsilon(t:y_c)]$											
Allegheny Airlines (1987)	0 to 10	−.21	.17	.14	.19	−.07	.08	−.01	−.05	.02	.05	.01
	−1 to −10		−.14	−.13	−.13	−.13	−.11	−.16	.10	.04	−.01	−.01
American Telephone &	0 to 10	−.07	.24	.23	.03	.17	−.14	−.13	.06	−.19	−.05	.13
Telegraph	−1 to −10		−.01	−.14	.08	−.28	.07	−.04	.11	−.01	.17	.17
Avco	0 to 10	.25	−.04	−.09	−.06	.03	−.22	−.25	.09	−.20	−.16	.28
	−1 to −10		.45	.08	.10	.08	.09	−.12	−.10	.03	.04	−.10

Gulf & Western	0 to 10	.08	−.14	.01	.21	.13	−.13	.05	.16	.06	.15	.07
	−1 to −10		−.06	.01	−.04	.00	−.02	−.14	.01	.07	.08	−.06
Loews	0 to 10	−.16	.16	−.07	.15	.11	−.03	.14	.03	.13	.06	.34
	−1 to −10		−.16	−.32	.00	−.35	−.22	−.17	.01	−.06	−.03	−.20
Northwest	0 to 10	−.48	−.18	.25	.01	−.16	−.08	−.10	−.03	.14	.22	.12
	−1 to −10		−.17	−.12	−.05	−.16	−.03	−.01	−.23	−.03	.03	.01
Tenneco	0 to 10	−.22	−.02	.04	−.02	.24	−.09	.28	.02	.21	−.04	.14
	−1 to −10		−.18	−.09	−.14	−.16	.00	.00	.22	.01	.03	.04
Trans World Airlines	0 to 10	.07	−.03	.02	.02	−.01	.01	−.05	.11	−.03	.11	.11
	−1 to −10		.06	.10	−.05	−.07	.05	.03	.12	.04	.00	.09
(c) Estimated Cross Correlation Function $r_k[\varepsilon(t:P_3);\ \varepsilon(t:y_c)]$												
Allegheny Airlines (1987)	0 to 10	−.02	.09	−.14	−.06	−.07	.00	.07	−.06	−.18	.00	.04
	−1 to −10		−.03	−.20	.09	.12	−.16	−.05	.08	.01	−.03	.06
American Telephone & Telegraph	0 to 10	.00	.09	−.24	−.09	.18	.16	−.35	−.04	−.08	−.07	.17
	−1 to −10		.50	.11	−.10	.09	−.20	.06	.04	−.12	−.05	−.09
Avco	0 to 10	−.11	.05	.17	.01	.24	.07	.17	.01	.07	.14	.12
	−1 to −10		.31	.20	.09	−.16	.06	−.03	.00	−.05	−.01	−.05
Gulf & Western	0 to 10	.25	.01	−.14	−.07	−.23	−.10	−.09	−.31	−.23	−.10	−.19
	−1 to −10		.36	.17	.19	.12	.03	.16	.13	.01	−.18	.11
Loews	0 to 10	−.03	.02	.06	−.16	.20	.08	.03	.13	−.05	.01	−.03
	−1 to −10		−.38	−.01	−.23	.05	.16	−.11	−.04	−.07	.11	−.12
Northwest	0 to 10	.25	−.11	.30	.16	−.20	−.01	.10	.19	−.07	.11	.12
	−1 to −10		.35	.13	−.02	.33	.08	−.08	.11	.08	.13	−.10
Tenneco	0 to 10	−.14	−.04	.00	−.07	−.08	−.20	−.04	−.02	−.34	.15	.12
	−1 to −10		−.02	.06	−.03	.01	−.02	.19	−.06	.15	.04	.09
Trans World Airlines	0 to 10	−.20	.13	.04	−.18	.16	−.01	−.04	.12	−.06	.03	.02
	−1 to −10		−.17	−.12	.00	−.09	−.15	.01	−.17	.04	.03	.01

price change. The majority of the correlations $r_k[\varepsilon(t:P_3); \varepsilon(t:y_c)]$ are large compared to their standard errors at lag $k = -1$.

Behavioral Dynamic Equations

As discussed in the introduction to Chapter 5, rational lag functions enable us to test a wide range of dependence structures between variables. Utilizing this idea, the model (5.3) can be extended in a natural way to provide for multiple inputs $i = 1, \ldots, M$:

$$(6.1a) \qquad y(t) = \frac{\beta(B)}{\alpha(B)} x_f(t) + \sum_{i=1}^{M} \frac{\beta^{(i)}(B)}{\alpha^{(i)}(B)} z_i(t) + \varepsilon(t),$$

where $y(t)$ is the option value for period t, $x_f(t)$ is one of the focus values at period t, $z_i(t)$ represents M exogenous variables, $\alpha^{(i)}(B)$ and $\beta^{(i)}(B)$ denote finite degree polynomials of unknown order, and $\varepsilon(t)$ is white noise. Equation (6.1a) is equivalent to

$$\begin{aligned}(6.1b) \quad y(t) = & \sum_{s=1}^{a} \alpha_s y(t-s) + \sum_{s=0}^{b} \beta_s x_f(t-s) \\ & + \sum_{s=1}^{a^{(1)}} \alpha_s^{(1)} y(t-s) + \sum_{s=0}^{b^{(1)}} \beta_s^{(1)} z_1(t-s) + \cdots \\ & + \sum_{s=1}^{a^{(M)}} \alpha_s^{(M)} y(t-s) + \sum_{s=0}^{b^{(M)}} \beta_s^{(M)} z_M(t-s) + \varepsilon(t).\end{aligned}$$

This section summarizes the results of efficiently fitting identified forms of (6.1) to the warrant data. All models are estimated assuming the basic expectations form (5.14). This represents a necessary step toward constructing a general model for warrant price changes. The format of the tabled results remains the same as explained at the beginning of the section on dynamic equations and will not be repeated here.

The Methodology

There are many different approaches that may be adopted in choosing which variables should be included in regression models. A criterion commonly employed for judging the importance of an additional variable is the partial correlation coefficient. A similar stepwise procedure does not exist for multi-input dynamic models. Here model building must allow for the specification of variable interrelationships. Adding another input involves specifying not only its rational lag function but also changing the nature of the rational lag functions of the other variables already included.

In the warrant data above, for example, the original exogenous variables were intercorrelated.

For these reasons, identification of (6.1) for the warrant data will proceed using the principal components of the section on results of principal components analysis as inputs rather than the original exogenous variables. The results of the section on independence of principal components indicate that these new dimensions are independent of each other. When the inputs are independent, one can directly identify an approximate form of a multi-input dynamic model. In this case, cross correlation estimates are helpful in indicating which variables should be added and how their rational lag functions should be characterized. Dependence may still exist between any one of these inputs and the focus values, but multivariate identification has clearly been made tractable. The experimental design is set up in the following way.

1. Two-stage identification can be used to specify one-input models for each principal component/warrant change pair. For bond usable warrants, include a model for the bond price/warrant change pair. Initial estimates for each pair can be obtained as explained in Chapter 3 in the discussion of parameter estimation.

2. Combine the parts of each pair to form a multivariate model.

3. The model identified at step two can now be efficiently fitted by conditional least squares. Diagnostic checks are used in the same way as for the one variable model, only here the statistics $S(+\text{lag})$ and $S(-\text{lag})$ must be inspected for each variable.

4. Continue the fitting and diagnostic checking until an acceptable model is obtained.

5. Incorporate the model fitted at step four and the fitted fundamental model of Chapter 5 into a behavioral model for the warrant pricing process. Include the simplest of the two noise models.

6. Fit the multivariate model identified at step five, using the nonlinear least squares routine. Initial parameter estimates used in the iterative estimation method are the efficient estimates obtained for each separate model.

7. Continue the fitting and diagnostic checking until an acceptable model is obtained.[5]

5. Although there are situations in which the models at step four may be of financial interest, the concern of this study is with how the model at step four can be parsimoniously combined with the fundamental dynamic models of Chapter 5 to identify a behavioral dynamic model for warrant price changes.

An Example

The model-building procedure outlined above will now be illustrated by continuing the example for Avco Corporation started in Chapter 5. It is now desired to examine how the focus high series $x_h(t)$, the three principal components $P_1(t)$, $P_2(t)$ and $P_3(t)$, and the bond series $z_5(t)$ for Avco might be related to the warrant series $y_c(t)$. The available data for each of the series consist of monthly values from March 1969 to September 1973.

Combining the Inputs

The patterns of the cross correlation estimates for the inputs of Avco in Tables 14(e) and 18 lead one to consider the multivariate model

$$(6.2)\quad y_c(t) = \beta_0^{(1)}P_1(t) + \beta_0^{(2)}P_2(t+1) + \beta_0^{(3)}P_3(t+1) + \beta_0^{(4)}z_5(t) + \varepsilon(t).$$

After shifting the second and third principal component series backward one month, the following fitted model was obtained:

$$(6.3)\qquad \begin{aligned} y_c(t) &= \underset{(.011)}{.026}P_1(t) + \underset{(.018)}{.054}P_2(t+1) + \underset{(.019)}{.020}P_3(t+1) \\ &\quad + \underset{(.005)}{.016}z_5(t) + \varepsilon(t) \\ \hat{\sigma}^2\varepsilon(t) &= .1108\text{E–}01 \qquad (49\text{df}). \end{aligned}$$

The residual autocorrelations do not indicate inadequacy, but residual cross correlations are somewhat large with $r_{-1}[\varepsilon(t{:}P_1);\varepsilon(t)] = -.43$, $r_{-2}[\varepsilon(t{:}P_1);\varepsilon(t)] = .29$, and $r_1[\varepsilon(t+1{:}P_2);\varepsilon(t)] = .28$. These terms are now added to the form (6.3) and the marginally significant parameter $\hat{\beta}_0^{(3)} = .020$ is dropped. After shifting the first principal component series backward two months, a further application of the nonlinear fitting procedure yielded

$$(6.4)\qquad \begin{aligned} y_c(t) &= (\underset{(.009)}{.022} - \underset{(.010)}{.025}B + \underset{(.010)}{.029}B^2)P_1(t+2) \\ &\quad + (\underset{(.016)}{.057}) + \underset{(.016)}{.028})P_2(t+1) + \underset{(.005)}{.016}z_5(t) + \varepsilon(t) \\ \hat{\sigma}^2\varepsilon(t) &= .9009\text{E–}02 \qquad (46\text{df}). \end{aligned}$$

Residual and cross correlation checks do not reveal further model inadequacy.

Adding the Fundamental Dynamic Model

Now by incorporating (6.4) and the fitted expectations equation (5.12), a behavioral model of the form

$$
\begin{aligned}
(6.5) \qquad y_c(t) = {} & (.492 + .688B - .264B^7)x_h(t+1) \\
& + (.022 - .025B + .029B^2)P_1(t+2) \\
& + (.057 + .028B)P_2(t+1) + .016z_5(t) + \varepsilon(t)
\end{aligned}
$$

is specified and a fitted model obtained:

$$
\begin{aligned}
(6.6) \qquad y_c(t) = {} & \underset{(.121)}{(5.13} + \underset{(.121)}{.655B} - \underset{(.092)}{.217B^7})x_h(t+1) \\
& + (\underset{(.007)}{.020} - \underset{(.007)}{.038B} + \underset{(.007)}{.017B^2})P_1(t+2) \\
& + (\underset{(.015)}{.016} - \underset{(.014)}{.001B})P_2(t+1) - \underset{(.005)}{.002z_5(t)} + \varepsilon(t)
\end{aligned}
$$

$$\hat{\sigma}^2\varepsilon(t) = .5034\text{E–}02 \qquad (45\text{df}).$$

Note that the coefficients on the expectations variable have remained nearly the same, while coefficients for the other inputs have changed as a result of their interaction with the expectations variable. The coefficients $\hat{\beta}_0^{(2)} = .016$, $\hat{\beta}_1^{(2)} = -.001$, and $\hat{\beta}_0^{(3)} = -.002$ are not large in comparison with their standard errors and can be dropped for later analysis.

Further Modeling

No model inadequacy is revealed by the cross correlation checks, but the estimation above was carried out under the assumption of uncorrelated disturbances. The estimated autocorrelations of the residuals found in Table 20(a) exhibit a pattern suggestive of a moving average process; i.e.,

$$(6.7) \qquad \varepsilon(t) = \frac{n(t)}{(1 - .400B^4)}.$$

TABLE 20

DIAGNOSTIC CHECKS FOR AVCO EXAMPLE OF BEHAVIORAL DYNAMIC MODEL

LAGS	0	1	2	3	4	5	6	7	8	9	10	Q
(a) ESTIMATED AUTOCORRELATION FUNCTION $r_k[\varepsilon(t)]$												
0 to 10	1.00	−.11	−.13	.10	−.35	.02	.25	−.15	.25	.08	−.04	16.50
11 to 20		.07	.05	−.08	.04	−.13	−.06	.08	−.06	−.08	.13	20.10
21 to 30		−.12	−.08	.03	−.11	−.05	.10	−.10	.10	.02	−.10	24.09

LAGS	0	1	2	3	4	5	6	7	8	9	10	S
(b) ESTIMATED CROSS CORRELATION FUNCTION $r_k[\varepsilon(t+1:x_h);n(t)]$												
0 to 10	−.04	−.07	−.01	−.14	.09	.16	−.17	−.02	.29	.10	−.20	11.73
11 to 20		.00	.18	−.19	−.05	.11	−.05	.01	−.02	−.11	−.10	17.23
21 to 30		.24	.02	−.26	−.19	−.04	.04	.15	−.01	−.11	.08	28.00
−1 to −10		.03	.15	.17	−.16	.02	.17	−.23	−.04	.09	−.07	9.02
−11 to −20		.11	.11	−.08	−.24	.15	.24	−.13	−.10	−.06	−.02	19.18
−21 to −30		−.08	−.06	−.06	.02	−.06	−.06	−.04	−.02	.01	−.01	20.36

LAGS	0	1	2	3	4	5	6	7	8	9	10	Q
(c) ESTIMATED AUTOCORRELATION FUNCTION $r_k[n(t)]$												
0 to 10	1.00	−.11	−.13	.16	.05	.03	.21	−.16	−.06	.14	.06	8.05
11 to 20		−.05	.02	−.04	.05	−.09	−.10	−.06	−.11	−.01	.03	10.22
21 to 30		−.17	−.14	−.01	.02	−.07	−.04	−.08	.04	−.01	−.07	13.57

LAGS	0	1	2	3	4	5	6	7	8	9	10	S
(d) ESTIMATED AUTOCORRELATION FUNCTION $r_k[\varepsilon(t+2:P_1);n(t)]$												
0 to 10	−.02	−.09	−.11	−.03	.07	.18	.20	−.02	.06	.02	.09	5.60
11 to 20		−.07	.08	.00	−.07	.14	−.20	.14	−.02	−.06	−.03	10.71
21 to 30		−.01	.01	−.08	.01	−.16	.03	.02	.14	−.29	−.02	17.85
−1 to −10		.12	−.03	−.03	−.20	−.01	.28	−.12	−.18	−.06	−.06	9.70
−11 to −20		−.04	−.11	−.14	−.01	.18	−.16	−.01	−.03	.13	−.07	15.63
−21 to −30		.02	−.01	.10	−.09	.09	.01	.14	.00	−.04	.05	18.29

One final application of the iterative least squares procedure gives the behavioral equation

$$
\begin{aligned}
(6.8)\quad y_c(t) = {} & \underset{(.064)}{(.630} + \underset{(.066)}{.670B} - \underset{(.064)}{.242B^7})x_h(t+1) \\
& + (\underset{(.006)}{.017} - \underset{(.006)}{.038B} + \underset{(.006)}{.015B^2})P_1(t+2) + \frac{n(t)}{(1 + \underset{(.125)}{.577B^4})}
\end{aligned}
$$

$$\hat{\sigma}^2 n(t) = .3737\text{E–}02 \qquad (45\text{df}).$$

The usual residual auto- and cross-correlation checks for up to 30 lags as shown in Tables 20(b), (c), and (d) indicate a good data fit.

Summary of the Avco Model

It appears that our modeling process has been helpful in indicating an appropriate multivariate model for the Avco data. The noise variance has again been reduced from .2178E–01 to .7883E–02 and now to .3737E–02. Thus, the step-by-step procedure utilizing independent principal components has developed a behavioral structure for the pricing of Avco's warrant. Figure 12 graphs the final fitted model (6.8) after converting the price changes back to normalized prices and plotting them against the actual normalized warrant series.

Results for Focus High

Table 21 reports the multivariate models fitted by nonlinear estimation techniques employing the focus high. Residual autocorrelations for each model are given in Table 22.

As can be seen from Table 21, combination of the fundamental dynamic models and the input variables works remarkably well in accounting for the structure of warrant price changes. Of the three principal components considered, only the psychological market factor (PMF) significantly enters into all but one equation. The PMF at period $(t + 1)$ enters with a negative coefficient in seven of the eight equations. At period t, only four warrants are positively related to the PMF. In general, the net effect (or sum) of these coefficients negatively influences the warrant pricing process.

The second component does not enter into any of the equations. As in the example for Avco, once the inputs are appended to the fundamental models, any comparison of volatility and volume has been accounted for by the focus high. The third component enters significantly and positively for the model of American Telephone and Telegraph and the model of

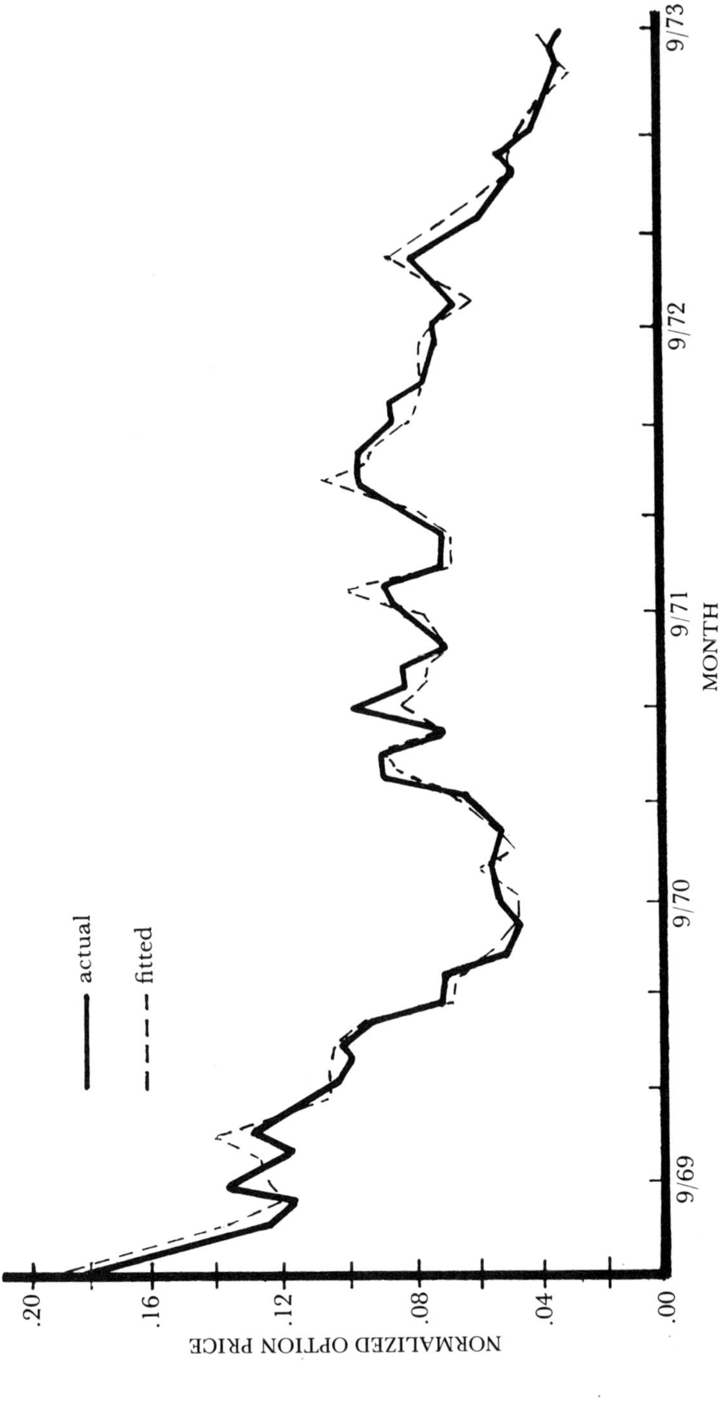

Fig. 12 Fitted behavioral dynamic model for Avco example

TABLE 21
BEHAVIORAL DYNAMIC MODELS FOR FOCUS HIGH

WARRANT	FITTED MODELS	RESIDUAL VARIANCE	df	DW
Allegheny Airlines (1987)	$y_c(t) = (\underset{(.093)}{.342} + \underset{(.116)}{.993}B - \underset{(.089)}{.285}B^2)x_h(t+1) + (-\underset{(.007)}{.023} + \underset{(.007)}{.030}B)P_1(t+1) + (1 - .618B)n(t)$	.8400E–02	67	1.766
American Telephone & Telegraph	$y_c(t) = (\underset{(.248)}{.870} + \underset{(.289)}{.544}B)x_h(t+1) + (\underset{(.009)}{.026} - \underset{(.008)}{.020}B)P_1(t) + (\underset{(.016)}{.040} + \underset{(.014)}{.026}B)P_3(t+1) + n(t)$	.4059E–02	31	2.156
Avco	$y_c(t) = (\underset{(.064)}{.630} + \underset{(.066)}{.670}B - \underset{(.064)}{.242}B^7)x_h(t+1) + (\underset{(.006)}{.017} - \underset{(.006)}{.038}B + \underset{(.006)}{.015}B^2)P_1(t+2) + \frac{n(t)}{(1 + \underset{(.125)}{.577}B^4)}$	.3737E–02	45	2.181
Gulf & Western	$y_c(t) = (\underset{(.127)}{.391} + \underset{(.127)}{.804}B)x_h(t+1) + (-\underset{(.008)}{.017} + \underset{(.008)}{.017}B)P_1(t+1) + .023P_3(t+1) + \frac{n(t)}{(1 + \underset{(.116)}{.421}B)}$	.9213E–02	60	1.792

Note: Standard errors are shown by parameter estimates. Residual variances are expressed in real exponential form. Degrees of freedom are denoted by df, and DW denotes the Durbin and Watson statistic.

(continued)

TABLE 21 *Continued*

WARRANT	FITTED MODELS	RESIDUAL VARIANCE	df	DW
Loews	$y_c(t) = (\underset{(.128)}{.771} + \underset{(.129)}{.681}B)x_h(t+1) + \dfrac{n(t)}{(1 + \underset{(.127)}{.714}B + \underset{(.138)}{.403}B^2)}$	.9068E–02	52	2.088
Northwest	$y_c(t) = (\underset{(.221)}{.726} + \underset{(.203)}{1.063}B)x_h(t+1) - \underset{(.012)}{.029}P_1(t+1) + (\underset{(.006)}{-.012} + \underset{(.006)}{.008}B)z_5(t+1) + (1 - \underset{(.157)}{.395}B)n(t)$	.7618E–02	38	1.967
Tenneco	$y_c(t) = (\underset{(.156)}{.684} + \underset{(.145)}{.796}B + \underset{(.144)}{.229}B^3)x_h(t+1) + (\underset{(.006)}{-.029} + \underset{(.006)}{.015}B^3)P_1(t+1) - \underset{(.004)}{.011}z_5(t+1) + (1 - \underset{(.151)}{.412}B)n(t)$	.3702E–02	44	1.881
Trans World Airlines	$y_c(t) = (\underset{(.076)}{.538} + \underset{(.076)}{.958}B + \underset{(.050)}{.158}B^5)x_h(t+1) - \underset{(.004)}{.017}P_1(t+1) + (\underset{(.002)}{-.005} + \underset{(.002)}{.004}B - \underset{(.002)}{.008}B^3)z_5(t+1) + (1 - \underset{(.065)}{.680}B)n(t)$	.9458E–02	131	2.184

TABLE 22
RESIDUAL AUTOCORRELATIONS FOR FOCUS HIGH MODELS FITTED IN TABLE 21

WARRANT	LAGS	1	2	3	4	5	6	7	8	9	10
Allegheny Airlines (1987)	1 to 10	.10	−.07	−.09	−.15	−.02	−.01	.13	.21	−.06	−.04
	11 to 20	.05	−.07	−.02	.02	.12	.08	−.09	−.01	.04	.02
American Telephone &	1 to 10	.09	−.15	.16	−.02	−.13	.11	.13	−.19	.10	−.11
Telegraph	11 to 20	.17	.01	−.01	.18	.16	.05	.02	.09	−.12	.06
Avco	1 to 10	−.11	−.13	.16	.05	.03	.22	−.16	−.06	.14	.06
	11 to 20	−.05	.02	−.04	.05	−.09	−.10	−.06	−.11	−.01	.03
Gulf & Western	1 to 10	.06	−.03	.03	−.03	−.10	.11	.18	−.11	−.04	−.06
	11 to 20	.03	.08	.08	−.01	−.06	−.08	−.07	.20	.02	−.09
Loews	1 to 10	−.06	−.07	−.15	.24	−.05	−.03	−.04	−.08	−.06	−.17
	11 to 20	.02	−.20	.12	−.09	.05	−.09	.22	−.08	.04	.11
Northwest	1 to 10	.01	.02	−.01	−.19	.05	.00	.27	.05	−.08	−.06
	11 to 20	−.20	−.04	.05	.25	.01	−.04	−.17	−.14	−.04	−.04
Tenneco	1 to 10	.01	−.10	.11	.19	−.09	−.21	.13	.10	−.04	.02
	11 to 20	.28	.00	.04	.20	.09	−.13	−.02	.03	−.05	−.14
Trans World Airlines	1 to 10	−.08	.05	.10	−.03	.12	.01	−.05	−.10	.12	−.07
	11 to 20	.10	.03	−.18	.01	.13	−.12	.12	−.03	−.23	.09

Gulf and Western. Investors appear to be examining trade-offs between the risk attributes of the American Telephone and Telegraph warrant and its stock. Price changes of Gulf and Western's warrant appear to be affected by one-month-ahead levels of warrant trade volume. Only for three of the six bond usable warrants is the change in bond prices significant. The sum of the coefficients is negative for all three.

Diagnostic Checks

Model fit seems to be good. The average reduction in residual variance is 23.4 per cent and 28.6 percent for NYSE warrants, and 18.2 percent for those listed on the ASE. Both the residual autocorrelations and the Durbin–Watson statistics are inconclusive with respect to autocorrelation. The quantities Q, $S(+\text{lag})$ and $S(-\text{lag})$ for the first 30 lags are displayed in Table 23. Comparison of these with χ^2 tables for specified degrees of freedom provides no grounds for questioning the models. It is interesting to note that the value $Q = 41.5$ for Trans World Airlines has been reduced from 49.2. One possible explanation may be that the behavioral model permits market interactions that make it possible for the slope of the fitted model to change with respect to any of the inputs. This could account for the "bend" in the warrant-common relation as maturity approaches. (See Figure 1.)

Results for Focus Low

Estimated multi-input models that include the focus low are shown in Table 24. Listed in Table 25 are the residual autocorrelations for each model.

The first principal component significantly enters into six of the models. Only five of these six equations, however, contain the PMF at period t, and each has a positive coefficient. Again, the second component has failed to appear in any of the equations. The third principal component of Gulf and Western, which entered the focus high model, is not significant and was deleted. For American Telephone and Telegraph, the third dimension now dominates, causing the PMF to be dropped completely. The bond price is significant for four of the bond usable warrants.

The equations developed for the focus lows are moderately good. The average reduction in the variance of the residuals is 21.6 percent and 12.7 percent for NYSE and ASE warrants respectively. Neither the residual autocorrelation nor the Durbin–Watson statistics disclose autocorrelation. Diagnostic checks, which are given in Table 26, provide no evidence that the models are inadequate.

TABLE 23
DIAGNOSTIC CHECKS FOR FOCUS HIGH MODELS FITTED IN TABLE 21

		x_h		P_1		P_3		z_5	
WARRANT	Q	$S(+\text{lag})$	$S(-\text{lag})$	$S(+\text{lag})$	$S(-\text{lag})$	$S(+\text{lag})$	$S(-\text{lag})$	$S(+\text{lag})$	$S(-\text{lag})$
Allegheny Airlines (1987)	16.2	19.5	34.6	18.0	28.4	—	—	—	—
American Telephone & Telegraph	12.5	14.9	9.8	20.8	15.6	13.5	20.6	—	—
Avco	13.6	28.0	20.4	17.8	18.3	—	—	—	—
Gulf & Western	16.0	19.5	27.2	19.7	16.4	29.7	22.0	—	—
Loews	21.7	17.2	13.2	—	—	—	—	—	—
Northwest	15.0	23.6	13.6	15.8	27.2	—	—	17.8	13.0
Tenneco	18.5	24.4	11.8	22.5	9.6	—	—	21.3	12.2
Trans World Airlines	41.5	20.9	20.7	19.9	23.3	—	—	34.0	29.8

TABLE 24
BEHAVIORAL DYNAMIC MODELS FOR FOCUS LOW

WARRANT	FITTED MODELS	RESIDUAL VARIANCE	df	DW
Allegheny Airlines (1987)	$y_c(t) = (\underset{(.105)}{.680} + \underset{(.104)}{.606}B)x_l(t+1) + \underset{(.008)}{.021}P_1(t) + .030z_5(t) + \dfrac{n(t)}{(1 + \underset{(.115)}{.328}B + \underset{(.124)}{.458}B^2)}$	.1141E–01	67	2.154
American Telephone & Telegraph	$y_c(t) = (\underset{(.301)}{1.671} + \underset{(.316)}{.594}B)x_l(t+1) + (\underset{(.015)}{.062} + \underset{(.015)}{.027}B)P_3(t+1) + n(t)$	.4051E–02	33	2.356
Avco	$y_c(t) = (\underset{(.093)}{.585} + \underset{(.090)}{.595}B + \underset{(.092)}{.202}B^5 - \underset{(.091)}{.254}B^7)x_l(t+1) + (\underset{(.007)}{.018} - \underset{(.008)}{.017}B + \underset{(.008)}{.028}B^2)P_1(t+2) + n(t)$	.5387E–02	45	2.279
Gulf & Western	$y_c(t) = (\underset{(.115)}{.619} + \underset{(.114)}{.607}B)x_l(t+1) + \dfrac{n(t)}{(1 + \underset{(.115)}{.419}B)}$	.1112E–01	63	1.935
Loews	$y_c(t) = (\underset{(.129)}{.617} + \underset{(.124)}{.592}B)x_l(t+1) + (\underset{(.011)}{.019} - \underset{(.012)}{.026}B^3)P_1(t+2) + (1 - \underset{(.142)}{.477}B)n(t)$	.1040E–01	50	1.766

Northwest	$y_c(t) = \underset{(.141)}{(.363} + \underset{(.151)}{.482B)}x_l(t+1) + \underset{(.015)}{.057}P_1(t) + \underset{(.007)}{(.015} - \underset{(.006)}{.016B)}z_5(t) + \dfrac{n(t)}{(1 + \underset{(.161)}{.331B})}$	.8842E–02	39	1.986
Tenneco	$y_c(t) = \underset{(.185)}{(.690} + \underset{(.155)}{.675B)}x_l(t+1) + (\underset{(.006)}{-.019} + \underset{(.007)}{.013B} + \underset{(.006)}{.013B^3})P_1(t+1) - \underset{(.004)}{.014}z_5(t+1) + (1 - \underset{(.148)}{.463B})n(t)$	.3833E–02	44	1.908
Trans World Airlines	$y_c(t) = \underset{(.078)}{(.786} + \underset{(.074)}{.691B)}x_l(t+1) + \underset{(.005)}{.016}P_1(t) + (\underset{(.002)}{-.008} + \underset{(.002)}{.003B})z_5(t+1) + (1 - \underset{(.067)}{.666B})n(t)$	.1029E–01	132	2.177

Note: Standard errors are shown by parameter estimates. Residual variances are expressed in real exponential form. Degrees of freedom are denoted by df, and DW denotes the Durbin and Watson statistic.

TABLE 25

RESIDUAL AUTOCORRELATIONS FOR FOCUS LOW MODELS FITTED IN TABLE 24

WARRANT	LAGS	1	2	3	4	5	6	7	8	9	10
Allegheny Airlines (1987)	1 to 10	−.09	−.02	−.19	.01	.03	−.01	.09	.12	−.06	−.07
	11 to 20	.08	.08	.03	−.04	−.07	−.04	−.05	.02	.07	.01
American Telephone & Telegraph	1 to 10	−.16	.08	−.06	.12	−.24	.07	−.06	.12	.14	−.09
	11 to 20	.25	−.10	−.05	−.15	.31	−.08	.14	−.10	.11	.08
Avco	1 to 10	−.14	−.11	−.05	−.23	.17	.06	.07	−.12	−.01	−.04
	11 to 20	.01	.12	−.06	.16	−.09	−.09	.14	−.18	−.09	.10
Gulf & Western	1 to 10	.01	−.14	−.11	.03	.01	.01	.00	−.28	.07	−.01
	11 to 20	−.03	−.08	.00	.03	.16	.08	−.11	.05	−.05	−.01
Loews	1 to 10	.00	.03	.03	.15	−.15	−.14	.03	−.10	−.12	−.20
	11 to 20	.03	−.20	.09	.03	.06	−.08	.23	−.09	−.05	.02
Northwest	1 to 10	−.01	−.01	.09	−.09	.06	−.11	.04	.04	−.16	−.05
	11 to 20	−.08	−.10	.17	.12	.06	−.01	−.07	−.07	.00	−.02
Tenneco	1 to 10	.01	−.04	.06	.07	−.07	−.07	−.09	.01	.08	−.14
	11 to 20	.29	.01	.06	.09	.10	.09	.01	−.05	−.09	−.08
Trans World Airlines	1 to 10	−.08	.08	.11	−.01	.05	−.02	.04	−.11	−.03	−.11
	11 to 20	.08	.01	.01	.01	.16	−.02	.09	.02	−.06	.08

TABLE 26
DIAGNOSTIC CHECKS FOR FOCUS LOW MODELS FITTED IN TABLE 24

WARRANT	Q	x_l S(+lag)	x_l S(−lag)	P_1 S(+lag)	P_1 S(−lag)	P_3 S(+lag)	P_3 S(−lag)	z_5 S(+lag)	z_5 S(−lag)
Allegheny Airlines (1987)	16.5	19.7	28.9	25.7	27.5	—	—	26.5	29.0
American Telephone & Telegraph	17.6	8.4	18.4	—	—	9.4	17.2	—	—
Avco	20.4	23.6	22.1	22.9	11.2	—	—	—	—
Gulf & Western	20.3	24.4	16.0	—	—	—	—	—	—
Loews	17.7	19.6	16.2	23.6	12.3	—	—	—	—
Northwest	8.9	16.5	20.0	28.0	6.4	—	—	17.4	20.8
Tenneco	15.2	14.0	14.6	17.5	10.9	—	—	24.7	13.5
Trans World Airlines	21.5	24.2	27.3	22.3	18.2	—	—	29.2	26.5

Discussion of Results and Conclusions

The above results have demonstrated that one can construct behavioral dynamic models for warrant price changes within the framework of multivariate rational lag models. Evidence as to the quality of fit achieved by appending variables to the fundamental equations can be obtained from a comparison of residual variances. The average reduction in the variance of the residuals from the models of Chapter 5 is 23.4 percent and 17.3 percent for the focus high and focus low respectively.

Several implications can be drawn from the results concerning the warrant pricing process.

1. A problem that sometimes impairs successful interpretation of multivariate model results is multicollinearity. This exists when some or all of the exogenous variables are highly collinear. The main consequence of multicollinearity is to cause variance to be arbitrarily allocated to the exogenous variables. In terms of the effect of multicollinearity on estimated coefficients, standard errors tend to be high and parameters can sometimes change abruptly when model identifications are even slightly modified.

To provide a basis for assessing the degree of multicollinearity in the behavioral dynamic equation, matrices of correlations among the exogenous variables have been computed.[6] As correlation between pairs of variables approaches 1.0 and -1.0, multicollinearity will be more pronounced. From these matrices, the numbers of correlations with a value $\geqq |0.4|$ or $\geqq |0.6|$ have been tabulated for all warrants as follows:

	Number of Correlations		Total Number of
	$\geqq \|0.4\|$	$\geqq \|0.6\|$	Correlations
Focus High Models	12	0	146
Focus Low Models	8	0	100

Also, from these matrices, the means of the absolute values of the lower hand, off diagonal correlations have been computed for each warrant:

Warrant	Focus High Models	Focus Low Models
Allegheny Air (1987)	0.18	0.16
American Telegraph and Telephone	0.12	0.17
Avco	0.13	0.12

6. Tests for the presence of multicollinearity require the use of various correlation coefficients, and procedures currently available can only indicate the variables most affected. [In this regard, see Johnson (1972).]

Gulf & Western	0.14	0.16
Loews	0.18	0.21
Northwest	0.18	0.17
Tenneco	0.14	0.15
Trans World Airlines	0.12	0.11
Average	0.15	0.16

To the extent that these correlations can suggest the degree of multicollinearity, it can be concluded that there is little evidence of multicollinearity for the behavioral dynamic equations.

2. Investors continually strive to obtain and interpret market information concerning the nature of the economy. Clearly related to the economic state of affairs in the near future are the anticipated conditions in the nation's money and capital markets. The major conclusion of the above results is that warrant investment decisions are seldom made without reference to general market conditions.

Of the three principal components, the first one clearly dominates the equations. As indicated in the section on principal components, this dimension can be interpreted as a psychological market factor (PMF). This term represents some factor which influences the pricing process of all warrants, but not necessarily to exactly the same extent. More simply, this dimension represents the various kinds of information flowing into the market, such as political news, unemployment figures, price index reports, etc., that are reflected in the price changes of warrants. Part of the PMF could also be generated internally in the market. A price change in one warrant could influence changes in other warrants, and these changes could influence the whole market.

3. The importance of interest rate risk appears to be supported by the data. Of the eight equations in Table 24, which contained the senior security variable, market prices were reduced by interest rate risk in seven of these as evidenced by the negative sign of the coefficients. This is clearly consistent with our earlier arguments.

Most of our data cover the period 1967–73, during which time the coupon rates on the senior securities were generally below the market interest rate levels. This period began just after the "credit crunch" of 1966–67, when corporations experienced a liquidity crisis and corporate bond yields jumped upward. Falling bond prices created by record yields did not attract funds into bonds. The period since 1967 has been characterized not only by pervasive tightness in the money and bond markets, but also by accelerated inflation. This has particular relevance to the bond markets after 1967 because yields steadily increased in the early part of this period. Later in the post-1967 period, a reverse trend became apparent as investors, discouraged by the inflationary spiral, moved out of the bond markets. Under these conditions, one should expect bond usable warrants to be priced lower than comparable warrants.

4. It is interesting that the average reduction in residual variance for the focus high models is 23.4 percent, while for the focus low models it is only 17.3 percent. This implies that the series of actual price changes can be fitted more precisely by accounting for investor perception of profit. Now why should this be?

It is commonly acknowledged that the appeal of options for speculators lies in their leverage. If the stock underlying the option rises sharply in price, the move would be magnified many times over in the option. But leverage works both ways. It generally takes a sizable upward move in the price of the stock for the buyer of options just to recoup his purchase price and transaction costs, let alone make a profit. There have not been many such moves in the slumping stock market of recent years, which might explain the relatively large percentage reduction for the focus low models.

5. A difference in goodness of fit appears, depending on which exchange the warrant is traded—when all other things are equal. For the focus high models, the average reduction in residual variance for NYSE warrants is 28.6 percent, whereas for ASE warrants it is 18.2 percent. Similarly, for the models fitted with the focus low, the average reduction in residual variance is 21.6 percent and 12.7 percent respectively. This agrees with the findings of Leabo and Rogalski (1974b). They observed that price movements of warrants exhibited different characteristics, depending on which of the major exchanges a warrant is traded. Douglas (1969) also concluded that the greatest portion of price variability was associated with the exchange on which the security is traded.

6. The coefficients $\hat{\beta}_0$, $\hat{\beta}_1$ of the behavioral dynamic equations have been averaged over all eight warrants. These are presented below in comparison with the average coefficients of the fundamental dynamic equations (shown in parentheses).

	$\hat{\beta}_0$	$\hat{\beta}_1$
Focus High Models	.567	.941
	(.582)	(.918)
Focus Low Models	.734	.722
	(.732)	(.618)

It is apparent that the coefficients $\hat{\beta}_0$, $\hat{\beta}_1$ have not substantially changed. This supports the conviction held throughout this study that the primary determinant of option price behavior is investor expectation of stock price.

Summary

The contention of this chapter has been that expectations alone do not explain warrant price changes. In this respect, various price determinant hypotheses were tested. It was concluded that trading volume for both the warrant and the stock plus the senior security of bond usable warrants positively influence changes in warrant price. Further investigation indicated the presence of collinearity among the determinants, although bond price changes were not dependent upon any of the other factors.

The results of a principal components analysis were both interesting and suggestive. Each of the components permitted straightforward identification of meaningful dimensions. In addition, no affirmative indication of dependence among components could be found. An examination of cross correlation estimates revealed that the first component (a general psychological market factor) and the third component (volatility trade-off) influenced the warrant pricing process.

Finally, behavioral dynamic equations were specified by combining relevant hypotheses. Each of the equations was efficiently fitted by a conditional least squares approach. Evidence as to quality of fit achieved was obtained from (a) residual variance reduction, and (2) residual auto- and cross correlation checks. The outcome of this analysis is that expectational variables play a greater role in warrant price formation than was previously recognized.

7

SUMMARY AND SUGGESTIONS FOR FUTURE RESEARCH

Summary

This analysis of the options market has suggested that models of option price behavior will not generally be successful in describing data unless they take account of both expectational variables and market interrelationships over time. A behavioral dynamic equation was developed on this premise, given a few general assumptions about investor behavior. Using this equation, it was shown that the rational lag model of Box–Jenkins could be used to derive testable equations of various expectational hypotheses. The results of the data analysis (1) confirm the hypothesis that changing investor expectations of stock prices are positively related to option price changes, and (2) support the hypotheses that psychological forces in the market plus interest rate risk are important price determinants.

In conclusion, three inferences can be drawn from the dynamic equations regarding option price behavior. These inferences, however, are drawn only from the experience of a limited sample of one type of option. Accepting this limitation, the major implications can be stated as follows: (1) when the information set available to investors is only historical prices, the random walk provides an adequate explanation of *monthly* option price changes; (2) when the information set is extended to include anticipated events, it is necessary to include more than just investor expectations of stock prices to explain option price changes; and (3) these additional speculative factors plus expectations can be effectively aggregated (including their interrelationships) by utilizing multivariate rational lag models.

Suggestions for Further Research

This research has provided many insights into option price behavior. It has also exposed areas conducive to further inquiry. Suggestions for further research are of two types: those that could be considered additions to the present study and those that would require a major effort. Extensions to this study might be made in the following areas:

1. Use of dynamic option price equations and the empirical test procedures to examine options other than warrants.
2. Use of refined proxies for the focus outcomes, and application of those values within the context of dynamic equations.
3. Testing the selected models on weekly data. Additional option price determinants could also be incorporated into the equations.
4. Examination of the underlying distributions of the option price and exogenous series. The statistical methods that were utilized here were based on the assumption that the time series under consideration were jointly stationary and normally distributed. [In this regard, see Leabo and Rogalski (1973).]
5. Development and testing of more complex option models, such as multiple equation time series models. Here, attention has been centered upon single equation models. The analysis might be improved by examining the simultaneous nature of market relations. [In this regard, see Hannan (1970).]

Research of a more difficult nature is dominated by a single topic: the study of investor behavior and/or expectations in an experimental situation. There have been many studies of market phenomena, but all of these have been essentially concerned with the behavior of price. If one knew more about human response to economic stimuli, one might come to a better understanding of price behavior. One must never lose sight of the fact that the behavior of people ultimately determines the behavior of price.

APPENDIXES

APPENDIX A

MEANS, STANDARD DEVIATIONS, AND COEFFICIENTS OF VARIATION OF DATA SERIES

Series	Mean	Standard Deviation	Standard Error of Mean
	Allegheny Airlines (1987)		
y_c	−.01042	.12955	.01516
x_c	−.01285	.16875	.01962
x_h	−.01400	.15474	.01798
x_l	−.00896	.14322	.01665
z_1	331.56	291.57	33.668
z_2	1703.5	1394.2	160.99
z_3	.03570	.01441	.00166
z_4	.02877	.00921	.00106
SS	60.103	6.7827	.78320
	American Telephone & Telegraph		
y_c	−.00107	.01681	.00272
x_c	.00297	.03970	.00644
x_h	.00311	.04103	.00665
x_l	.00311	.03200	.00519
z_1	15107.	4434.1	1810.2
z_2	18677.	4918.6	2008.0
z_3	.02367	.00438	.00179
z_4	.01095	.00181	.00074
	Avco		
y_c	−.00307	.01249	.00170
x_c	−.00818	.03893	.00529
x_h	−.00885	.03615	.00492
x_l	−.00815	.03181	.00433
z_1	2714.8	1507.1	435.07
z_2	4400.0	3246.3	937.13
z_3	.03216	.00700	.00203
z_4	.01800	.00458	.00132
SS	84.750	4.8535	1.4011
	Gulf & Western		
y_c	−.00353	.02533	.00309
x_c	−.00407	.06552	.00800
x_h	−.00712	.06457	.00788

(*continued*)

Series	Mean	Standard Deviation	Standard Error of Mean
	Gulf & Western—*continued*		
x_l	−.00365	.05215	.00642
z_1	5315.8	2802.2	808.92
z_2	8519.5	2251.3	649.89
z_3	.03288	.01166	.00336
z_4	.02606	.00847	.00244
	Loews		
y_c	−.01261	.07413	.00981
x_c	−.01233	.12359	.01637
x_h	−.01461	.12056	.01597
x_l	−.00886	.10466	.01386
z_1	5628.6	2807.5	371.86
z_2	5144.5	3611.4	478.34
z_3	.03495	.01275	.00168
z_4	.02494	.01547	.00205
SS	78.222	6.1142	.80284
	Northwest		
y_c	.00369	.06806	.01033
x_c	.00717	.09456	.01394
x_h	.00608	.07503	.01106
x_l	.00423	.09526	.01405
z_1	1709.7	1120.0	165.13
z_2	394.28	1772.1	261.28
z_3	.06495	.19489	.02873
z_4	.02703	.01143	.00168
SS	80.992	8.0809	1.1915
	Tenneco		
y_c	−.00315	−.00222	.00308
x_c	−.00121	−.05476	.00759
x_h	−.00144	−.04905	.00680
x_l	−.00356	−.04504	.00625
z_1	1197.0	645.36	89.496
z_2	6924.9	3278.9	454.70
z_3	.02835	.00925	.00128
z_4	.01294	.00456	.00063
SS	85.399	6.0487	.83085
	Trans World Airlines		
y_c	−.00064	.20119	.01700
x_c	.00276	.23832	.02014
x_h	.00291	.23672	.02006
x_l	.00171	.21343	.01804
z_1	5919.7	7539.2	634.92
z_2	5555.3	4300.9	362.20
z_3	.03519	.01727	.00145
z_4	.02559	.01018	.00086
SS	85.238	16.475	1.3874

APPENDIX B

ESTIMATED AUTOCORRELATIONS FOR PRICE SERIES

Series	1	2	3	4	5	6	7	8	9	10
140 obs					Allegheny Corporation					
y_c	−.01	.00	−.03	.12	−.11	−.11	−.08	−.07	−.01	−.08
x_c	.02	−.01	−.01	.14	−.13	−.12	−.12	−.07	.00	−.08
x_h	.09	.04	.04	.02	−.13	−.09	−.08	−.09	−.06	−.03
x_l	.19	−.02	−.04	.04	.01	−.05	−.22	−.17	.05	.07
140 obs					Atlas					
y_c	−.10	−.08	−.06	.21	−.03	−.02	−.14	−.08	.05	.05
x_c	−.12	.00	−.08	.22	−.03	.00	−.11	−.08	−.02	−.05
x_h	−.01	−.10	−.05	.12	.06	−.01	−.11	−.06	−.13	.00
x_l	.03	−.10	−.05	.12	.11	−.03	−.06	−.03	−.01	.02
45 obs					Bluebird					
y_c	.02	.11	.06	−.13	.22	−.09	.14	−.20	−.12	.09
x_c	.02	−.04	−.17	−.22	.34	−.09	.00	−.27	−.23	.12
x_h	.21	.00	−.23	.06	−.02	−.04	−.22	−.12	−.33	.05
x_l	.25	−.11	−.23	−.18	.17	.09	−.03	−.21	−.33	−.10
64 obs					Braniff					
y_c	−.05	−.04	.09	.10	−.02	.06	−.01	.07	.04	−.09
x_c	−.06	−.04	.01	.08	−.02	.02	.02	.13	.03	−.03
x_h	−.03	.00	.10	.07	−.05	.03	.11	.04	.04	.06
x_l	−.01	−.15	.06	.08	.07	.10	.09	.24	.03	.12
36 obs					Brown					
y_c	.03	−.19	.05	−.09	−.11	−.19	−.01	.08	−.12	−.01
x_c	−.07	−.23	.08	−.07	−.09	−.19	.04	.02	−.07	−.09
x_h	−.03	−.12	.00	−.13	−.15	−.01	−.12	.02	−.06	−.04
x_l	.02	−.05	−.28	−.12	−.11	.01	.06	−.05	−.09	.00
40 obs					Continental Telephone					
y_c	−.31	.02	−.04	.10	−.18	.06	−.02	.01	−.25	.12
x_c	−.16	−.02	.06	.02	−.26	.03	−.06	−.06	−.11	.04
x_h	.13	.17	.09	−.26	−.10	−.26	−.19	.09	−.18	.15
x_l	.01	.00	.09	−.12	−.11	−.13	.07	−.28	−.05	.15

(continued)

SERIES	1	2	3	4	5	6	7	8	9	10
49 OBS					ELGIN					
y_c	−.08	−.12	.06	−.04	.15	−.07	−.17	.01	−.09	−.03
x_c	.11	−.21	−.12	.03	.03	−.10	−.03	−.14	−.09	.14
x_h	.06	.04	−.13	−.07	.01	.00	−.07	−.05	.08	.19
x_l	.12	−.08	.03	−.07	−.04	−.09	.03	−.07	−.09	−.09
49 OBS					FIBREBOARD					
y_c	.12	.09	−.03	−.10	.04	.12	−.13	−.04	−.21	−.18
x_c	.10	−.01	−.23	−.15	.04	.19	.02	−.14	−.35	−.08
x_h	.21	−.02	−.19	−.15	.12	.14	−.15	−.19	−.28	−.15
x_l	.21	−.09	.00	−.22	−.15	.21	.07	−.30	−.22	−.09
32 OBS					FLYING TIGER					
y_c	−.03	.04	−.06	.00	−.25	.09	−.06	.00	−.13	.02
x_c	.11	.06	−.09	.04	−.28	−.07	−.15	−.05	−.12	.08
x_h	.10	.23	−.11	−.03	−.31	−.03	−.23	−.01	−.14	.09
x_l	.10	.02	−.07	.03	−.14	−.06	−.18	−.11	−.02	.13
71 OBS					FRONTIER AIRLINES					
y_c	−.08	−.03	.02	.11	−.08	−.19	.20	−.20	−.10	−.15
x_c	−.06	.02	−.04	.14	−.03	−.19	.17	−.17	−.09	−.23
x_h	.09	−.07	.08	.09	−.15	−.10	−.02	−.09	−.15	−.11
x_l	.00	−.11	−.04	.28	−.10	−.14	.04	.06	−.28	−.05
98 OBS					INDIAN HEAD					
y_c	−.05	.15	−.07	.13	.05	.03	−.04	−.07	−.05	−.07
x_c	.04	−.05	−.09	.17	.02	−.08	−.05	−.08	−.03	−.04
x_h	.08	.05	−.03	.09	.04	.02	−.11	−.08	−.07	−.02
x_l	.15	−.20	.04	.09	.07	−.03	−.06	−.07	−.18	.06
42 OBS					KANE-MILLER					
y_c	−.01	.00	−.16	.20	−.23	−.08	−.22	.05	.02	.13
x_c	.14	.04	−.04	.01	−.32	−.09	−.29	−.07	.03	.13
x_h	.22	−.02	.07	−.24	−.17	−.06	−.21	−.17	.15	.09
x_l	.21	.25	−.03	−.12	−.19	−.34	−.18	−.11	−.11	.10
53 OBS					LEASCO					
y_c	.09	.08	−.04	−.03	−.22	−.12	.05	−.16	−.01	.02
x_c	.16	.06	−.05	.06	−.08	−.09	−.03	−.18	.02	−.03
x_h	.08	−.12	.10	−.03	−.02	−.03	−.12	.05	−.15	−.02
x_l	.23	.06	.03	.01	−.11	.00	.06	−.19	−.12	−.02
64 OBS					LERNER					
y_c	.08	−.16	−.08	.01	−.05	.07	.01	−.29	−.01	.06
x_c	−.31	.07	−.23	.00	.18	.03	.12	−.26	.12	−.18
x_h	−.15	−.01	−.40	−.05	.32	.10	.05	−.25	−.03	.02
x_l	−.13	−.09	−.22	.01	.07	.24	−.01	−.04	−.24	.12

Series	1	2	3	4	5	6	7	8	9	10
134 obs					McCrory (1976)					
y_c	.02	−.09	.00	.05	.05	.14	.04	−.08	−.09	−.05
x_c	.02	−.02	.04	−.09	.09	.01	.12	.06	−.09	−.05
x_h	.21	.00	−.03	−.04	.15	.01	.06	−.03	−.06	−.06
x_l	.12	−.09	−.02	.06	.03	.07	.18	−.05	−.10	−.07
88 obs					McCrory (1981)					
y_c	.14	−.16	−.07	−.03	.21	.13	−.09	−.15	−.10	−.02
x_c	.03	.05	.02	−.11	.10	−.13	.11	−.01	−.16	−.02
x_h	.21	.03	−.02	−.05	.10	−.03	−.01	−.15	−.12	−.04
x_l	.16	−.02	.05	.00	−.08	−.05	.10	.00	−.18	−.04
106 obs					National General (1974)					
y_c	.02	.06	−.02	.03	.07	.05	.15	−.09	−.01	−.02
x_c	−.08	.08	−.13	.02	.15	.09	.16	−.23	.07	−.05
x_h	.16	−.09	−.07	.09	.24	.20	.06	−.04	−.16	.08
x_l	.19	−.03	−.10	.09	.20	.17	.08	−.16	−.10	.13
58 obs					National General (1978)					
y_c	−.04	.12	.06	.13	−.01	.08	.16	−.24	−.03	.00
x_c	−.24	.12	−.16	.09	.17	.07	.14	−.25	.05	−.12
x_h	.04	−.05	.07	.11	.21	.24	−.01	−.10	−.15	.14
x_l	.19	−.11	−.11	.10	.20	.20	.12	−.17	−.22	.13
57 obs					National Industries					
y_c	.09	.03	−.01	.20	−.03	−.07	.10	−.04	−.06	−.05
x_c	.01	.02	−.06	.20	−.04	.00	.07	−.15	−.05	.00
x_h	.13	−.18	.10	.18	.10	−.13	.03	.09	−.10	−.04
x_l	.23	.12	.06	.10	.10	−.12	.18	−.04	−.14	−.01
36 obs					Northern Natural Gas					
y_c	.05	−.13	.18	.01	−.14	−.17	−.05	.02	−.22	.04
x_c	−.08	.08	.01	−.02	−.09	−.02	−.03	.06	−.24	.02
x_h	−.06	.02	.27	−.36	.19	−.05	−.13	.17	−.22	−.10
x_l	−.02	.00	.19	−.27	−.02	.08	−.04	−.15	.14	−.05
62 obs					P.S.A.					
y_c	−.06	.18	−.14	.13	−.08	−.11	.04	−.29	.13	−.08
x_c	−.06	.18	−.03	−.03	−.10	−.18	−.03	−.27	.00	.00
x_h	.10	.17	.01	−.07	−.12	−.13	−.24	−.14	.00	.02
x_l	.10	−.07	.08	−.07	−.11	−.07	−.07	−.20	.00	.20
72 obs					Textron					
y_c	.03	−.11	−.08	.12	.10	.00	−.10	−.03	−.03	.06
x_c	−.03	−.01	−.15	.19	.00	.01	−.06	.03	−.06	.06
x_h	.11	−.10	.02	.15	.06	.02	−.08	.05	.01	.01
x_l	.04	−.07	−.04	.09	.11	.02	−.03	−.09	.01	.12

(continued)

Series	1	2	3	4	5	6	7	8	9	10
120 obs					Uris					
y_c	−.02	.13	.11	−.04	.10	.09	.00	−.08	−.01	−.04
x_c	−.04	.06	.00	−.03	.11	.03	.08	−.16	.02	−.08
x_h	.17	−.01	.16	−.04	.06	.13	−.06	−.11	−.05	.00
x_l	.09	−.04	.09	−.05	.06	.09	.01	−.16	.07	.04
47 obs					U.V. Industries					
y_c	−.05	−.06	−.11	.26	−.26	−.09	.11	−.04	−.28	−.19
x_c	−.01	−.19	−.05	.11	−.08	.02	.08	−.08	−.32	−.12
x_h	.10	−.13	−.18	.15	−.04	−.01	.07	−.13	−.37	−.03
x_l	.16	−.15	−.05	.14	−.19	−.05	.09	−.20	−.31	−.18
55 obs					Ward					
y_c	.20	−.09	−.23	−.08	.10	.05	−.07	−.14	−.01	.17
x_c	.04	.04	−.19	−.09	−.10	.18	.02	−.14	−.20	.15
x_h	.06	−.05	−.08	−.20	.06	.11	−.06	−.08	−.24	.02
x_l	.14	−.06	−.05	−.22	−.06	.01	.06	−.13	−.09	.12
52 obs					Whittaker					
y_c	−.08	.00	−.02	.06	−.09	−.15	.25	−.02	.06	−.16
x_c	.05	−.14	−.05	.17	−.03	−.14	.15	.01	−.02	−.16
x_h	.10	−.30	.09	.12	−.04	−.11	.10	.12	−.16	−.06
x_l	.17	.08	.08	.10	−.14	.07	.08	−.02	−.09	−.03
32 obs					Williams Cos.					
y_c	−.05	−.10	.01	−.09	−.02	−.08	−.24	.07	.11	.12
x_c	−.04	−.10	−.13	−.03	−.12	−.02	−.22	.12	.12	.15
x_h	.11	.09	−.33	−.18	−.15	−.02	−.02	−.18	.15	.15
x_l	.13	−.12	−.21	−.23	.00	−.25	−.07	.20	.01	.26

APPENDIX C

RELATIONSHIPS BETWEEN PRICE AND FOCUS VALUE FOR OPTION POPULATIONS

Series*	Lags	0	1	2	3	4	5	6	7	8	9	10
140 obs						Allegheny Corporation						
$r_k[\varepsilon(t:x_c); \varepsilon(t:y_c)]$	0 to 10	.95	.04	−.05	−.01	.16	−.10	−.15	−.08	−.10	.00	−.07
	−1 to −10		−.01	.05	−.04	.10	−.14	−.08	−.12	−.03	−.01	−.09
$r_k[\varepsilon(t:x_h); \varepsilon(t:y_c)]$	0 to 10	.76	−.10	.07	.02	.09	−.23	−.04	−.11	−.11	.06	−.04
	−1 to −10		.33	.05	−.01	.05	−.09	−.10	−.07	−.03	−.08	−.07
$r_k[\varepsilon(t:x_l); \varepsilon(t:y_c)]$	0 to 10	.47	.07	−.13	.10	.02	−.02	−.15	−.10	−.13	−.03	.11
	−1 to −10		.61	.00	.01	−.02	.01	−.07	−.10	−.18	−.06	−.06
140 obs						Atlas						
$r_k[\varepsilon(t:x_c); \varepsilon(t:y_c)]$	0 to 10	.75	−.01	.04	−.09	.19	−.01	.03	−.15	−.05	.01	−.01
	−1 to −10		−.06	−.06	−.02	.17	−.02	−.07	−.08	−.08	.01	−.01
$r_k[\varepsilon(t:x_h); \varepsilon(t:y_c)]$	0 to 10	.65	−.04	−.03	.00	.14	.04	−.06	−.09	−.13	.08	.01
	−1 to −10		.16	−.07	−.07	.14	−.01	−.02	−.12	.00	−.11	.00
$r_k[\varepsilon(t:x_l); \varepsilon(t:y_c)]$	0 to 10	.40	.00	−.11	.09	.11	−.06	.00	−.08	−.01	−.05	.07
	−1 to −10		.39	−.08	−.04	.06	.22	−.08	−.07	−.10	.03	−.07
45 obs						Bluebird						
$r_k[\varepsilon(t:x_c); \varepsilon(t:y_c)]$	0 to 10	.70	.18	.07	−.01	−.24	.25	−.07	.12	−.22	−.28	.12
	−1 to −10		−.03	.07	−.20	−.13	.21	−.11	.06	−.26	−.09	.05
$r_k[\varepsilon(t:x_h); \varepsilon(t:y_c)]$	0 to 10	.58	.16	.14	−.15	.10	.07	−.02	−.06	−.32	−.18	.05
	−1 to −10		.40	−.03	−.14	−.11	.10	−.03	−.12	−.02	−.16	−.02
$r_k[\varepsilon(t:x_l); \varepsilon(t:y_c)]$	0 to 10	.36	.26	.02	−.10	.01	.03	.16	−.11	−.10	−.24	−.13
	−1 to −10		.54	.00	−.28	−.03	−.06	.12	.01	−.12	−.21	−.18

* Base variables are listed before the semicolon; cross variables are listed after it.

(continued)

Series	Lags	0	1	2	3	4	5	6	7	8	9	10
64 obs						Braniff						
$r_k[\varepsilon(t:x_c);\varepsilon(t:y_c)]$	0 to 10	.88	.07	−.06	.03	.14	−.02	−.02	−.04	.13	.04	−.18
	−1 to −10		−.19	.01	.07	.05	.02	.13	.07	.09	.07	.02
$r_k[\varepsilon(t:x_h);\varepsilon(t:y_c)]$	0 to 10	.67	−.01	−.09	.16	.18	−.15	.03	.07	.06	−.12	.13
	−1 to −10		.13	.06	.14	−.07	.05	.09	.05	.17	−.01	.04
$r_k[\varepsilon(t:x_l);\varepsilon(t:y_c)]$	0 to 10	.46	−.05	−.01	.12	−.04	.06	−.08	.13	.16	−.30	.08
	−1 to −10		.41	−.19	−.02	.11	.09	.02	.03	.20	.17	−.07
36 obs						Brown						
$r_k[\varepsilon(t:x_c);\varepsilon(t:y_c)]$	0 to 10	.95	−.03	−.19	.08	−.08	−.06	−.20	.00	.07	−.12	−.02
	−1 to −10		.03	−.23	.05	−.09	−.14	−.18	.04	.04	−.06	−.08
$r_k[\varepsilon(t:x_h);\varepsilon(t:y_c)]$	0 to 10	.90	−.09	−.15	.06	−.13	−.07	−.15	−.04	.09	−.16	.03
	−1 to −10		.17	−.14	−.01	−.09	−.21	−.04	−.10	.00	−.03	−.07
$r_k[\varepsilon(t:x_l);\varepsilon(t:y_c)]$	0 to 10	.16	−.01	−.09	−.08	.00	−.19	−.05	.03	−.09	−.01	.07
	−1 to −10		.78	−.03	−.15	−.10	−.15	−.23	.08	.10	−.02	−.14
40 obs						Continental Telephone						
$r_k[\varepsilon(t:x_c);\varepsilon(t:y_c)]$	0 to 10	.83	−.10	−.04	.05	.13	−.16	.00	−.02	−.09	−.10	−.03
	−1 to −10		−.26	.02	−.01	−.06	−.23	.05	−.01	.01	−.24	.17
$r_k[\varepsilon(t:x_h);\varepsilon(t:y_c)]$	0 to 10	.53	−.07	.06	.10	−.09	−.03	−.08	−.08	.01	−.23	.14
	−1 to −10		.25	.00	−.05	−.08	−.14	−.14	−.06	−.02	−.01	−.06
$r_k[\varepsilon(t:x_l);\varepsilon(t:y_c)]$	0 to 10	.55	−.10	−.02	.10	−.02	−.06	.03	−.03	−.19	−.14	.21
	−1 to −10		.20	−.10	−.02	.04	−.29	.04	−.02	.05	−.20	.07
49 obs						Elgin						
$r_k[\varepsilon(t:x_c);\varepsilon(t:y_c)]$	0 to 10	.25	.47	−.18	−.18	.00	.06	.16	−.04	−.16	−.28	−.13
	−1 to −10		−.19	−.03	−.03	.17	.02	−.14	.01	−.07	−.05	.06
$r_k[\varepsilon(t:x_h);\varepsilon(t:y_c)]$	0 to 10	.43	−.03	−.08	−.06	−.03	.09	.04	−.12	−.22	−.21	−.12
	−1 to −10		.34	−.36	.05	−.02	.08	.01	−.11	−.07	−.03	.02
$r_k[\varepsilon(t:x_l);\varepsilon(t:y_c)]$	0 to 10	.38	.11	−.11	.01	−.12	−.04	.07	.00	−.14	−.22	−.24
	−1 to −10		.06	−.21	.02	.11	.14	−.11	−.06	.03	−.02	.00

49 OBS						FIBREBOARD						
$r_k[\varepsilon(t:x_c); \varepsilon(t:y_c)]$	0 to 10	.79	.32	.03	−.03	−.09	.01	.26	.06	−.13	−.12	−.23
	−1 to −10		.02	.01	−.31	−.13	−.04	.01	−.08	−.07	−.29	.00
$r_k[\varepsilon(t:x_h); \varepsilon(t:y_c)]$	0 to 10	.73	.24	.08	−.10	.03	.14	.14	−.10	.01	−.30	−.13
	−1 to −10		.30	−.04	−.15	−.31	.01	.06	−.19	.00	−.34	−.11
$r_k[\varepsilon(t:x_l); \varepsilon(t:y_c)]$	0 to 10	.48	.19	.11	−.02	−.20	.21	.13	.00	−.14	−.24	−.10
	−1 to −10		.64	−.07	−.16	−.11	−.23	.02	−.01	−.17	−.23	−.10
32 OBS						FLYING TIGER						
$r_k[\varepsilon(t:x_c); \varepsilon(t:y_c)]$	0 to 10	.90	.02	.06	−.04	.03	−.26	−.02	−.05	−.08	−.12	.07
	−1 to −10		.12	.02	−.06	−.03	−.26	.05	−.13	.00	−.15	.07
$r_k[\varepsilon(t:x_h); \varepsilon(t:y_c)]$	0 to 10	.78	−.10	.11	−.10	−.06	−.27	.03	−.12	.00	−.08	−.02
	−1 to −10		.20	.34	−.10	−.02	−.25	.05	−.11	.01	−.27	.11
$r_k[\varepsilon(t:x_l); \varepsilon(t:y_c)]$	0 to 10	.65	.13	−.16	.12	−.13	−.20	.01	−.07	−.18	.07	−.03
	−1 to −10		.33	.13	−.19	.11	−.20	.04	−.09	−.03	−.16	.13
71 OBS						FRONTIER AIRLINES						
$r_k[\varepsilon(t:x_c); \varepsilon(t:y_c)]$	0 to 10	.83	.06	−.05	−.04	.16	−.02	−.18	.17	−.11	−.18	−.21
	−1 to −10		−.09	.05	−.01	.14	−.11	−.20	.23	−.27	−.01	−.17
$r_k[\varepsilon(t:x_h); \varepsilon(t:y_c)]$	0 to 10	.70	.04	−.09	.09	.17	−.12	−.12	.04	−.19	−.10	−.09
	−1 to −10		.16	.04	.05	.06	−.18	−.16	.16	−.13	−.09	−.16
$r_k[\varepsilon(t:x_l); \varepsilon(t:y_c)]$	0 to 10	.47	−.01	−.08	.16	.04	−.13	.06	.14	−.17	−.32	.05
	−1 to −10		.49	−.21	−.04	.13	.08	−.15	−.18	.16	−.20	−.03
98 OBS						INDIAN HEAD						
$r_k[\varepsilon(t:x_c); \varepsilon(t:y_c)]$	0 to 10	.83	.07	.03	−.03	.09	.09	−.02	.01	−.15	−.01	−.06
	−1 to −10		.02	.05	−.04	.15	.03	−.04	−.03	−.06	−.06	−.08
$r_k[\varepsilon(t:x_h); \varepsilon(t:y_c)]$	0 to 10	.64	.01	.02	.09	.10	.04	.04	−.12	−.07	−.03	−.03
	−1 to −10		.33	.10	.01	.00	.10	.05	−.05	−.02	−.14	−.09
$r_k[\varepsilon(t:x_l); \varepsilon(t:y_c)]$	0 to 10	.56	.00	−.06	.12	.06	.00	.05	−.06	−.17	−.03	.04
	−1 to −10		.42	.08	−.11	.07	.23	−.01	−.06	−.03	−.11	−.06

(continued)

Series	Lags	0	1	2	3	4	5	6	7	8	9	10
42 obs						Kane-Miller						
$r_k[\varepsilon(t:x_c);\varepsilon(t:y_c)]$	0 to 10	.90	.10	.01	−.07	.13	−.26	−.09	−.20	−.03	−.02	.11
	−1 to −10		.04	.03	−.11	.12	−.26	−.09	−.29	.01	.06	.16
$r_k[\varepsilon(t:x_h);\varepsilon(t:y_c)]$	0 to 10	.64	.16	−.11	.07	−.21	−.08	−.12	−.13	−.09	.11	.09
	−1 to −10		.41	−.10	.10	.02	−.24	−.04	−.23	−.10	.05	.15
$r_k[\varepsilon(t:x_l);\varepsilon(t:y_c)]$	0 to 10	.50	.08	.13	−.14	.01	−.33	−.08	−.12	−.07	−.02	.10
	−1 to −10		.56	.10	−.08	.02	−.05	−.16	.33	.00	−.06	.13
53 obs						Leasco						
$r_k[\varepsilon(t:x_c);\varepsilon(t:y_c)]$	0 to 10	.90	.12	.17	−.08	−.04	−.22	−.04	−.01	−.17	−.01	.02
	−1 to −10		.14	.03	.01	.05	−.08	−.14	.01	−.21	.01	−.01
$r_k[\varepsilon(t:x_h);\varepsilon(t:y_c)]$	0 to 10	.59	.02	.00	.07	−.18	−.11	−.04	−.03	−.01	−.12	.08
	−1 to −10		.51	−.06	.07	−.01	−.01	−.09	−.05	−.10	−.08	−.03
$r_k[\varepsilon(t:x_l);\varepsilon(t:y_c)]$	0 to 10	.51	.24	.07	.01	−.18	−.21	.08	−.02	−.08	−.11	.11
	−1 to −10		.58	−.10	.06	.08	.04	−.10	−.11	−.10	−.21	.11
64 obs						Lerner						
$r_k[\varepsilon(t:x_c);\varepsilon(t:y_c)]$	0 to 10	.66	−.19	−.10	.03	.07	.19	−.04	.10	−.37	.17	−.06
	−1 to −10		.01	.04	−.19	−.08	.01	.18	.06	−.25	−.01	−.15
$r_k[\varepsilon(t:x_h);\varepsilon(t:y_c)]$	0 to 10	.33	−.30	−.12	.06	.06	.32	−.18	.02	−.19	.15	.03
	−1 to −10		.27	.26	−.23	−.12	−.08	.23	.17	−.14	−.23	−.14
$r_k[\varepsilon(t:x_l);\varepsilon(t:y_c)]$	0 to 10	.23	−.21	−.10	.17	.06	.32	−.10	−.10	−.20	.10	.03
	−1 to −10		.40	.08	−.20	−.05	−.05	.08	.14	−.06	−.28	.00
134 obs						McCrory (1976)						
$r_k[\varepsilon(t:x_c);\varepsilon(t:y_c)]$	0 to 10	.82	.07	−.10	.06	−.07	.07	.04	.08	−.05	−.13	−.03
	−1 to −10		.07	−.05	−.01	.03	.07	.09	.05	.08	−.07	−.02
$r_k[\varepsilon(t:x_h);\varepsilon(t:y_c)]$	0 to 10	.57	.01	−.06	.01	.01	.13	−.02	.02	−.13	−.11	.06
	−1 to −10		.50	.01	−.07	−.01	.12	.05	.13	.07	−.05	−.06
$r_k[\varepsilon(t:x_l);\varepsilon(t:y_c)]$	0 to 10	.42	.00	.03	−.03	.02	.02	.10	.04	−.13	−.11	−.12
	−1 to −10		.52	−.01	−.14	.11	.12	.04	.09	.04	.02	−.07

88 OBS					McCRORY (1981)								
$r_k[\varepsilon(t:x_c);\ \varepsilon(t:y_c)]$	0 to 10	.80	.13	−.09	.03	−.08	.14	−.01	.02	−.05	−.18	−.09
	−1 to −10		.14	−.05	−.05	−.02	.12	.00	.00	−.02	−.11	.06
$r_k[\varepsilon(t:x_h);\ \varepsilon(t:y_c)]$	0 to 10	.59	.03	−.13	.04	.02	.16	−.07	−.06	−.11	−.14	.02
	−1 to −10		.52	.07	−.09	−.10	.11	.08	.11	−.10	−.18	−.05
$r_k[\varepsilon(t:x_l);\ \varepsilon(t:y_c)]$	0 to 10	.50	.02	.10	−.07	−.02	.05	.07	−.01	−.16	−.20	−.06
	−1 to −10		.50	−.02	−.10	.11	.04	.01	−.06	−.06	.05	−.03
106 OBS					NATIONAL GENERAL (1974)								
$r_k[\varepsilon(t:x_c);\ \varepsilon(t:y_c)]$	0 to 10	.85	.01	.19	−.04	.04	.07	.14	.09	−.10	.01	.00
	−1 to −10		−.02	−.04	−.09	.05	.15	−.01	.21	−.17	.06	−.06
$r_k[\varepsilon(t:x_h);\ \varepsilon(t:y_c)]$	0 to 10	.68	.04	.09	.13	.04	.04	.16	.03	−.07	−.05	.07
	−1 to −10		.33	−.10	−.06	.01	.25	.13	.08	.04	−.13	.04
$r_k[\varepsilon(t:x_l);\ \varepsilon(t:y_c)]$	0 to 10	.51	.13	.03	−.01	.03	.21	.13	−.01	−.14	.00	.11
	−1 to −10		.51	.00	−.10	.06	.06	.15	.06	.03	−.09	.02
58 OBS					NATIONAL GENERAL (1978)								
$r_k[\varepsilon(t:x_c);\ \varepsilon(t:y_c)]$	0 to 10	.75	−.10	.15	−.07	.14	.14	.22	.11	−.20	.02	.09
	−1 to −10		−.08	.16	−.17	.08	.02	.05	.16	−.24	.01	−.15
$r_k[\varepsilon(t:x_h);\ \varepsilon(t:y_c)]$	0 to 10	.51	−.03	.21	.17	.04	.27	−.04	−.19	.06	.12	−.07
	−1 to −10		.37	.04	−.05	.06	.07	.15	.12	.03	−.24	−.06
$r_k[\varepsilon(t:x_l);\ \varepsilon(t:y_c)]$	0 to 10	.52	−.05	−.02	.14	.10	.21	.20	.05	−.24	.01	.21
	−1 to −10		.53	.01	−.10	.04	.08	.05	.13	−.03	−.19	−.02
57 OBS					NATIONAL INDUSTRIES								
$r_k[\varepsilon(t:x_c);\ \varepsilon(t:y_c)]$	0 to 10	.86	.12	.02	−.12	.35	−.09	.04	−.01	.05	−.08	.05
	−1 to - 10		.07	−.01	.08	.02	.07	−.11	.18	−.18	−.05	−.04
$r_k[\varepsilon(t:x_h);\ \varepsilon(t:y_c)]$	0 to 10	.58	.05	−.21	.36	.12	−.01	−.12	.08	.05	.03	.04
	−1 to −10		.46	.06	−.09	.20	.04	−.09	.02	.18	−.25	.01
$r_k[\varepsilon(t:x_l);\ \varepsilon(t:y_c)]$	0 to 10	.44	.16	−.01	.26	.00	−.10	.13	.04	.01	.09	.19
	−1 to −10		.63	.01	.02	.15	.18	−.04	−.07	.10	−.22	.04

(continued)

Series	Lags	0	1	2	3	4	5	6	7	8	9	10
36 obs					Northern Natural Gas							
$r_k[\varepsilon(t{:}x_c);\ \varepsilon(t{:}y_c)]$	0 to 10	.88	.02	−.05	.21	.04	−.17	−.03	−.10	.14	−.19	.09
	−1 to −10		−.02	.00	.08	−.05	−.07	−.21	−.01	−.02	−.19	.00
$r_k(\varepsilon(t{:}x_h);\ \varepsilon(t{:}y_c)]$	0 to 10	.62	.04	.07	−.03	−.03	.07	−.33	.09	.13	−.31	.12
	−1 to −10		.26	−.10	.31	−.16	−.08	.12	−.27	.06	−.09	−.08
$r_k[\varepsilon(t{:}x_l);\ \varepsilon(t{:}y_c)]$	0 to 10	.55	−.04	.12	.05	−.14	−.01	−.05	−.06	.04	−.07	−.08
	−1 to −10		.45	−.12	.17	−.12	−.01	−.15	−.08	.01	−.13	.09
62 obs					P.S.A.							
$r_k[\varepsilon(t{:}x_c);\ \varepsilon(t{:}y_c)]$	0 to 10	.91	−.02	.18	−.14	.11	−.14	−.09	−.03	−.25	.07	−.03
	−1 to −10		−.05	.17	−.02	.01	−.08	−.14	.00	−.27	.04	−.03
$r_k[\varepsilon(t{:}x_h);\ \varepsilon(t{:}y_c)]$	0 to 10	.51	.13	.05	−.10	.05	−.11	−.14	−.11	−.03	.00	.11
	−1 to −10		.43	.15	.02	.00	−.04	−.06	−.19	−.05	−.26	.11
$r_k[\varepsilon(t{:}x_l);\ \varepsilon(t{:}y_c)]$	0 to 10	.49	.11	−.04	−.01	−.04	−.13	.00	−.11	−.07	−.04	.31
	−1 to −10		.53	−.09	.08	.05	.02	−.17	−.09	−.13	−.11	.09
72 obs					Textron							
$r_k[\varepsilon(t{:}x_c);\ \varepsilon(t{:}y_c)]$	0 to 10	.94	.06	−.07	−.14	.20	.04	.04	−.09	−.02	−.05	.07
	−1 to −10		.01	−.08	−.08	.10	.07	−.03	−.07	.02	−.03	.05
$r_k[\varepsilon(t{:}x_h);\ \varepsilon(t{:}y_c)]$	0 to 10	.61	−.06	−.11	.07	.14	.09	−.13	−.15	.16	−.01	−.05
	−1 to −10		.49	.05	−.14	.05	.13	.01	.03	−.04	−.09	.12
$r_k[\varepsilon(t{:}x_l);\ \varepsilon(t{:}y_c)]$	0 to 10	.67	−.05	−.07	−.02	.14	.00	.01	−.01	−.05	−.08	.05
	−1 to −10		.44	−.13	−.01	−.01	.11	.21	−.20	−.07	−.01	.19
120 obs					Uris							
$r_k[\varepsilon(t{:}x_c);\ \varepsilon(t{:}y_c)]$	0 to 10	.93	.03	.08	.04	−.01	.09	.04	.08	−.16	−.01	−.07
	−1 to −10		−.04	.11	.07	−.04	.11	.08	.01	−.08	.01	−.07
$r_k[\varepsilon(t{:}x_h);\ \varepsilon(t{:}y_c)]$	0 to 10	.66	.02	.09	.12	−.03	.15	.00	−.12	.04	−.19	.07
	−1 to −10		.43	.07	.12	−.01	.01	.14	.08	−.07	−.08	.02
$r_k[\varepsilon(t{:}x_l);\ \varepsilon(t{:}y_c)]$	0 to 10	.51	.02	.12	.01	−.03	.09	.15	−.11	−.17	.07	−.03
	−1 to −10		.53	−.02	.13	−.02	.00	.14	.03	−.07	−.03	.05

47 OBS						U.V. INDUSTRIES						
$r_k[\varepsilon(t:x_c); \varepsilon(t:y_c)]$	0 to 10	.85	.03	−.09	−.04	.14	−.20	−.02	.11	−.07	−.33	−.13
	−1 to −10		.00	−.12	−.12	.24	−.17	−.08	.13	−.07	−.31	−.15
$r_k[\varepsilon(t:x_h); \varepsilon(t:y_c)]$	0 to 10	.66	−.16	−.05	.05	−.04	−.17	.04	.07	−.22	−.31	.10
	−1 to −10		.43	−.03	−.28	.23	−.02	−.11	.01	.07	−.26	−.29
$r_k[\varepsilon(t:x_l); \varepsilon(t:y_c)]$	0 to 10	.51	.10	−.14	.15	−.05	−.32	.10	.09	−.19	.45	.18
	−1 to −10		.55	−.26	−.03	.07	.07	−.18	.05	−.07	−.25	−.21
55 OBS						WARD						
$r_k[\varepsilon(t:x_c); \varepsilon(t:y_c)]$	0 to 10	.77	.15	.09	−.19	−.09	−.01	.14	.08	−.16	−.27	.08
	−1 to −10		.05	.05	−.21	−.16	.00	.02	−.03	−.04	−.01	.21
$r_k[\varepsilon(t:x_h); \varepsilon(t:y_c)]$	0 to 10	.45	.12	−.05	−.16	−.04	.12	.15	−.15	−.24	−.08	−.03
	−1 to −10		.52	−.04	−.10	−.16	−.19	.11	.00	−.02	−.02	−.01
$r_k[\varepsilon(t:x_l); \varepsilon(t:y_c)]$	0 to 10	.54	.13	−.04	−.15	−.01	.00	.09	.00	−.08	−.07	.00
	−1 to −10		.35	.11	−.09	−.23	−.12	.05	−.02	−.06	−.09	.14
52 OBS						WHITTAKER						
$r_k[\varepsilon(t:x_c); \varepsilon(t:y_c)]$	0 to 10	.83	.14	−.13	−.09	.12	−.01	−.20	.24	.00	.01	−.19
	−1 to −10		−.08	.07	−.05	.19	−.12	−.13	.19	.00	.01	−.13
$r_k[\varepsilon(t:x_h); \varepsilon(t:y_c)]$	0 to 10	.74	−.05	−.20	.09	.10	−.21	−.06	.30	.03	−.22	.05
	−1 to −10		.26	−.09	.02	.02	.10	−.12	.06	.07	.02	−.11
$r_k[\varepsilon(t:x_l); \varepsilon(t:y_c)]$	0 to 10	.35	.16	−.11	.10	−.03	−.19	.17	.06	−.01	−.11	.02
	−1 to −10		.60	−.03	.04	.06	.13	−.14	−.04	.20	−.17	.09
32 OBS						WILLIAMS COS.						
$r_k[\varepsilon(t:x_c); \varepsilon(t:y_c)]$	0 to 10	.95	−.04	−.12	−.08	−.07	−.06	−.07	−.21	.11	.13	.19
	−1 to −10		−.02	−.09	−.05	−.01	−.10	−.03	−.24	.06	.13	.08
$r_k[\varepsilon(t:x_h); \varepsilon(t:y_c)]$	0 to 10	.68	−.06	−.05	−.27	−.02	−.12	−.06	−.11	.21	.13	.25
	−1 to −10		.32	.05	−.05	−.15	−.08	.07	−.28	−.09	.14	.11
$r_k[\varepsilon(t:x_l); \varepsilon(t:y_c)]$	0 to 10	.41	.08	−.25	−.07	−.08	−.11	−.26	−.06	.17	.15	.28
	−1 to −10		.48	−.13	−.19	.03	−.08	.01	−.18	−.01	.09	.13

SELECTED BIBLIOGRAPHY

Ayres, H. F. "Risk Aversion in the Warrant Markets." *Industrial Management Review* (Fall 1963): 45–54.

Bachelier, L. "Théorie de la speculation." Paris: Gouthier-Villars, 1900.

Black, F. "Fact and Fantasy in the Use of Options." *Financial Analysts Journal* 31 (1975): 36–72.

———, and Scholes, M. "The Pricing of Options and Corporate Liabilities." *Journal of Political Economy* 81 (1973): 637–54.

———. "The Valuation of Option Contracts and a Test of Market Efficiency." *Journal of Finance* 27 (1972): 399–417.

Boness, J. A. "Elements of a Theory of Stock-Option Value." *Journal of Political Economy* 72 (1964): 163–75.

Box, G. E. P., and Jenkins, G. M. *Time Series Analysis.* San Francisco: Holden-Day, 1970.

Burrell, O. K. "An Experiment in Speculative Behavior." Bureau of Business Research Pamphlet, University of Oregon, 1950.

Chen, A. H. Y. "A Model of Warrant Pricing in a Dynamic Market." *Journal of Finance* 25 (1970): 1041–59.

Chopra, K. K. "The Valuation of Warrants and the Effects of Maturity." Ph.D. dissertation, Cornell University, 1973.

Cootner, P. H., editor. *The Random Character of Stock Market Prices.* Cambridge, Mass.: M.I.T. Press, 1967.

Cox, J. C., and Ross, S. A. "The Pricing of Options for Jump Processes." Rodney L. White Center for Financial Research Working Paper 2-75, University of Pennsylvania, 1975.

———. "The Valuation of Options for Alternative Stochastic Processes." *Journal of Financial Economics* 3 (1976): 145–66.

Cragg, J. G., and Malkiel, B. G. "Expectations and the Structure of Share Prices." *American Economic Review* 60 (1970): 601–17.

Douglas, G. W. "Risk in the Equity Markets: An Empirical Appraisal of Market Efficiency." *Yale Economic Essays* (Spring 1969): 3–46.

Durbin, J. "Testing for Serial Correlation in Least Squares Regression When Some of the Regressors Are Lagged Dependent Variables." *Econometrica* 38 (1970): 410–21.

Egerton, R. A. D. *Investment Decisions Under Uncertainty.* Cambridge, England: Liverpool University Press, 1960.

Ezekiel, I. M. "The Cobweb Theorem." *Quarterly Journal of Economics* 52 (1938): 255–80.

Fama, E. F. "The Behavior of Stock Market Prices." *Journal of Business* 38 (1965): 34–105.

———. "Efficient Capital Markets: A Review of Theory and Empirical Work." *Journal of Finance* 25 (1970): 383–417.

———, and Miller, M. H. *The Theory of Finance.* New York: Holt, Rinehart, and Winston, 1972.

Fried, S. *The Speculative Merits of Common Stock Warrants.* New York: R.H.M. Associates, 1961.

Giguere, G. "Warrants: A Mathematical Method of Evaluation." *Analysts Journal* 14 (1958): 17–25.

Goloi, D., and Mosulis, R. W. "The Option Pricing Model and the Risk Factor of the Stock." *Journal of Financial Economics* 3 (1976): 53–82.

Goodwin, R. M. "Dynamic Coupling with Especial Reference to Markets Having Production Lags." *Econometrica* 15 (1947): 181–204.

Gould, J. P., and Goloi, D. "Transactions Costs and the Relationship between Put and Call Prices." *Journal of Financial Economics* 1 (1974): 105–29.

Granger, C. W. J., and Morgenstern, O. *Predictability of Stock Market Prices.* Lexington, Mass.: D.C. Heath and Company, 1970.

Griliches, Z. "Distributed Lags: A Survey." *Econometrica* 35 (1967): 16–49.

Hallingby, P. "Speculative Opportunities in Stock Purchase Warrants." *Analysts Journal* (Third Quarter 1947): 48–49.

Hannan, E. J. *Multiple Time Series.* New York: Wiley, 1970.

Haugh, L. D. "The Identification of Time Series Interrelationships with Special Reference to Dynamic Regression Models." Ph.D. dissertation, University of Wisconsin, 1972.

Hausman, W. H., and White, W. L. "Theory of Option Strategy Under Risk Aversion." *Journal of Financial and Quantitative Analysis* 31 (1968): 343–58.

Hsu, D. "Stochastic Instability and the Behavior of Stock Prices." Ph.D. dissertation, University of Wisconsin, 1973.

Johnson, J. *Econometric Methods.* New York: McGraw-Hill, 1972.

Jorgenson, D. W. "Rational Distributed Lag Functions." *Econometrica* 34 (1966): 135–49.

Kassouf, S. T. "A Theory and an Econometric Model for Common Stock Purchase Warrants." Ph.D. dissertation, Columbia University, 1965.

———. "Warrant Price Behavior—1945 to 1964." *Financial Analysts Journal* 24 (1968): 123–28.

Koyck, L. M. *Distributed Lags and Investment Analysis.* Amsterdam: North Holland Publishing Company, 1954.

Leabo, D. A. *Basic Statistics*, 5th ed. Homewood, Ill.: Richard Irwin Co., 1977.

———, and Rogalski, R. J. "The Distribution of Stock Purchase Warrant Price Changes." *1973 Proceedings: Business and Economic Statistics Section—American Statistical Association.* Washington, D.C., 1973.

———. "Warrant Price Movements and the Efficient Market Hypothesis." *Journal of Finance* 30 (Mar. 1975): 163–77.

Leonard, R. J. "An Empirical Examination of a New General Equilibrium Model for Warrant Pricing." M.S. thesis, M.I.T., 1971.

Mark, R. M. "A Statistical and Theoretical Analysis of Common Stock Purchase Options." Ph.D. dissertation, New York University, 1973.

Marquardt, D. W. "An Algorithm for Least Squares Estimation of Nonlinear Parameters." *Journal of Society of Industrial Applied Mathematics* 2 (1963): 431–41.

McGuigon, J. R. "Timing Strategies in the Call Option Market." Ph.D. dissertation, University of Pittsburgh, 1971.

Melicher, R. W., and Rush, D. F. "An Empirical Examination of Factors Which Influence Warrant Prices." *Journal of Finance* 29 (Dec. 1974): 1449–66.

Merton, R. C. "Option Pricing When Underlying Stock Returns Are Discontinuous." *Journal of Financial Economics* 3 (1976): 125–44.

———. "Theory of Rational Option Pricing." *Bell Journal of Economics and Management Science* (Spring 1973): 141–83.

———, and Samuelson, P. A. "A Complete Model of Warrant Pricing That Maximizes Utility." *Industrial Management Review* (Winter 1969): 17–46.

Miller, J. D. "Effects of Longevity on Values of Stock Purchase Warrants." *Financial Analysts Journal* 27 (1971): 78–85.

Moore, A. B. "A Statistical Analysis of Common Stock Prices." Ph.D. dissertation, University of Chicago, 1964.

Morrison, R. "The Warrants or the Stock." *Analysts Journal* 13 (1957): 51–52.

Muth, J. F. "Rational Expectations and the Theory of Price Movements." *Econometrica* 29 (1961): 315–35.

Nerlove, M. *The Dynamics of Supply: Estimation of Farmers' Response to Price.* Baltimore: Johns Hopkins Press, 1958.

Newbold, P. "On Time Series and Dynamic Regression." Ph.D. dissertation, University of Wisconsin, 1970.

Parkinson, M. "Empirical Warrant–Stock Relationships." *Journal of Business* 45 (1972): 563–69.

Pierce, D. A. "Residual Correlations and Diagnostic Checking in Dynamic Disturbance Time Series Models." *Journal of the American Statistical Association* 67 (1972): 636–40.

———. "Studies in Modeling of Stochastic and Dynamic Systems with Special Reference to the Distribution of Residual Correlations." Ph.D. dissertation, University of Wisconsin, 1968.

Rogalski, R. J. "Trading in Warrants by Mechanical Systems." *Journal of Finance* 32 (1977): 87–102.

Roll, R. "The Efficient Market Model Applied to U.S. Treasury Bill Rates." Ph.D. dissertation, University of Chicago, 1968.

Ross, S. A. "Options and Efficiency." *Quarterly Journal of Economics* 40 (1975): 75–89.

Rubinstein, M. "The Valuation of Uncertain Income Streams and the Pricing of Options." *Bell Journal of Economics* 7 (1976): 407–25.

Samuelson, P. A. "Proof That Properly Anticipated Prices Fluctuate Randomly." *Industrial Management Review* (Spring 1965b): 41–49.

———. "A Rational Theory of Warrant Pricing." *Industrial Management Review* (Spring 1965a): 13–31.

Sargent, T. J. "Rational Expectations and the Term Structure of Interest Rates." *Journal of Money, Credit and Banking* 4 (1972): 74–97.

Shackle, G. L. S. *Decision Time and Order in Human Affairs.* Cambridge, Mass.: The University Press, 1961.

———. *Expectations in Economics.* Cambridge, England: The University Press, 1949.

Sharpe, W. F. "Capital Asset Prices: A Theory of Market Equilibrium Under Conditions of Risk." *Journal of Finance* 19 (1964): 425–42.

———. *Portfolio Theory and Capital Markets.* New York: McGraw-Hill, 1970.

Shelton, J. P. "The Relation of the Price of a Warrant to the Price of Its Associated Stock." *Financial Analysts Journal* 23 (May–June 1967), 43–151; (July–August 1967), 88–99.

Sims, C. A. "Money, Income, and Causality." *American Economic Review* 62 (1972): 540–52.

Smith, C. W. "Option Pricing: A Review." *Journal of Financial Economics* 3 (1976): 3–52.

Sprenkle, C. "Warrant Prices as Indicators of Expectations and Preferences." *Yale Economic Essays* (Spring 1961): 178–231.

Stone, D. G. "A Price Model for Common Stock Warrants." Ph.D. dissertation, New York University, 1970.

Van Horne, J. C. "Warrant Valuation in Relation to Volatility and Opportunity Costs." *Industrial Management Review* (Spring 1969): 19–32.

Von Neuman, J., and Morgenstern, O. *Theory of Games and Economic Behavior.* New Jersey: Princeton University Press, 1947.

Weinraub, H. J. "Warrant Valuation in Rational Security Markets." Ph.D. dissertation, Michigan State University, 1972.

Working, H. "A Theory of Anticipatory Prices." *American Economic Review* 48 (1958): 188–99.